GLENCOE LANG[UAGE]

SPELLING POWER

GRADE 8

Glencoe
McGraw-Hill

New York, New York   Columbus, Ohio   Woodland Hills, California   Peoria, Illinois

To the Student

This *Spelling Power* workbook provides the practice you need to improve your spelling and writing ability and to expand your vocabulary. Each spelling lesson focuses on a single spelling pattern or concept that applies to a list of words in a Word Bank. You then have several opportunities to practice what you've learned: writing the words, using them in sentences, recognizing and correcting them as you proofread, and applying the spelling pattern or concept to new words that follow the same pattern. If you have trouble with an exercise, you can always go back to the Word Bank and Key Concepts discussion, review the material, and then return to the exercise.

You can keep track of your own progress and achievement in spelling by using the Student Progress Chart, which appears on page v. With your teacher's help, you can score your work on any lesson, quiz, or test. After you know your score, use the Scoring Scale on pages vi–vii to figure your percentage. Then mark your score (or percentage correct) on the Student Progress Chart. Share your Progress Chart with your parents or guardians as your teacher directs.

Glencoe/McGraw-Hill

A Division of The **McGraw·Hill** *Companies*

Copyright © by The McGraw-Hill Companies, Inc. All rights reserved. Except as permitted under the United States Copyright Act of 1976, no part of this publication may be reproduced or distributed in any form or means, or stored in a database or retrieval system, without the prior written permission of the publisher.

Send all inquiries to:
Glencoe/McGraw-Hill
8787 Orion Place
Columbus, Ohio 43240

ISBN 0-07-826242-9

Printed in the United States of America

10 024 09 08 07

CONTENTS

STUDENT PROGRESS CHART

Fill in the chart below with your scores, using the scoring scale on the next page.

Name: _____

	Lesson	Pretest	Oral Quiz	Unit Review
1				
2				
3				
4				
Review				
5				
6				
7				
8				
Review				
9				
10				
11				
12				
Review				
13				
14				
15				
16				
Review				
17				
18				
19				
20				
Review				
21				
22				
23				
24				
Review				
25				
26				
27				
28				
Review				
29				
30				
31				
32				
Review				

Use this scale to find your score. Line up the number of items with the number correct. For example, if 15 out of 16 items are correct, your score is 93.7 percent (see grayed area).

Number Correct

Number of Items

	1	2	3	4	5	6	7	8	9	10	11	12	13	14	15	16	17	18	19	20
1	100																			
2	50	100																		
3	33.3	66.7	100																	
4	25	50	75	100																
5	20	40	60	80	100															
6	16.7	33.3	50	66.7	83.3	100														
7	14.3	28.6	42.9	57.1	71.4	85.7	100													
8	12.5	25	37.5	50	62.5	75	87.5	100												
9	11.1	22.2	33.3	44.4	55.6	66.7	77.8	88.9	100											
10	10	20	30	40	50	60	70	80	90	100										
11	9.1	18.1	27.2	36.3	45.4	54.5	63.6	72.7	81.8	90.9	100									
12	8.3	16.7	25	33.3	41.7	50	58.3	66.7	75	83.3	91.7	100								
13	7.7	15.3	23.1	30.8	38.5	46.1	53.8	61.5	69.2	76.9	84.6	92.3	100							
14	7.1	14.3	21.4	28.6	35.7	42.8	50	57.1	64.3	71.4	78.5	85.7	92.8	100						
15	6.7	13.3	20	26.7	33.3	40	46.6	53.3	60	66.7	73.3	80	86.7	93.3	100					
16	6.3	12.5	18.8	25	31.2	37.5	43.7	50	56.2	62.5	68.7	75	81.2	87.5	93.7	100				
17	5.9	11.8	17.6	23.5	29.4	35.3	41.2	47	52.9	58.8	64.7	70.6	76.5	82.3	88.2	94.1	100			
18	5.6	11.1	16.7	22.2	27.8	33.3	38.9	44.4	50	55.5	61.1	66.7	72.2	77.8	83.3	88.9	94.4	100		
19	5.3	10.5	15.8	21.2	26.3	31.6	36.8	42.1	47.4	52.6	57.9	63.1	68.4	73.7	78.9	84.2	89.4	94.7	100	
20	5	10	15	20	25	30	35	40	45	50	55	60	65	70	75	80	85	90	95	100
21	4.8	9.5	14.3	19	23.8	28.6	33.3	38.1	42.8	47.6	52.3	57.1	61.9	66.7	71.4	76.1	80.9	85.7	90.5	95.2
22	4.5	9.1	13.7	18.2	22.7	27.3	31.8	36.4	40.9	45.4	50	54.5	59.1	63.6	68.1	72.7	77.2	81.8	86.4	90.9
23	4.3	8.7	13.0	17.4	21.7	26.1	30.4	34.8	39.1	43.5	47.8	52.1	56.5	60.8	65.2	69.5	73.9	78.3	82.6	86.9
24	4.7	8.3	12.5	16.7	20.8	25	29.2	33.3	37.5	41.7	45.8	50	54.2	58.3	62.5	66.7	70.8	75	79.1	83.3
25	4	8	12	16	20	24	28	32	36	40	44	48	52	56	60	64	68	72	76	80
26	3.8	7.7	11.5	15.4	19.2	23.1	26.9	30.4	34.6	38.5	42.3	46.2	50	53.8	57.7	61.5	65.4	69.2	73.1	76.9
27	3.7	7.4	11.1	14.8	18.5	22.2	25.9	29.6	33.3	37	40.7	44.4	48.1	51.9	55.6	59.2	63	66.7	70.4	74.1
28	3.6	7.1	10.7	14.3	17.9	21.4	25	28.6	32.1	35.7	39.3	42.9	46.4	50	53.6	57.1	60.7	64.3	67.9	71.4
29	3.4	6.9	10.3	13.8	17.2	20.7	24.1	27.6	31	34.5	37.9	41.4	44.8	48.3	51.7	55.2	58.6	62.1	65.5	69
30	3.3	6.7	10	13.3	16.7	20	23.3	26.7	30	33.3	36.7	40	43.3	46.7	50	53.3	56.7	60	63.3	66.7
31	3.2	6.5	9.7	13	16.1	19.3	22.3	25.8	29.0	32.2	35.4	38.7	41.9	45.1	48.3	51.6	54.8	58	61.2	64.5
32	3.1	6.3	9.4	12.5	15.6	18.8	21.9	25	28.1	31.3	34.4	37.5	40.6	43.8	46.9	50	53.1	56.2	59.4	62.5
33	3	6	9	12	15.1	18.1	21.2	24.2	27.2	30.3	33	36.3	39.3	42.4	45.4	48.4	51.5	54.5	57.5	60.6
34	2.9	5.9	8.8	11.8	14.7	17.6	20.6	23.5	26.5	29.4	32.4	35.3	38.2	41.2	44.1	47.1	50	52.9	55.9	58.8
35	2.9	5.7	8.6	11.4	14.3	17.1	20	22.9	25.7	28.6	31.4	34.3	37.1	40	42.9	45.7	48.6	51.4	54.3	57.1
36	2.8	5.6	8.3	11.1	13.9	16.7	19.4	22.2	25	27.8	30.6	33.3	36.1	38.9	41.7	44.4	47.2	50	52.7	55.6
37	2.7	5.4	8.1	10.8	13.5	17.1	18.9	21.6	24.3	27	29.7	32.4	35.1	37.8	40	43.2	45.9	48.6	51.4	54
38	2.6	5.3	7.9	10.5	13.2	15.8	18.4	21.1	23.7	26.3	28.9	31.6	34.2	36.8	39.5	42.1	44.7	47.4	50	52.6
39	2.6	5.3	7.7	10.3	12.8	15.4	17.9	20.5	23.1	25.6	28.2	30.8	33.3	35.9	38.5	41.0	43.6	46.2	48.7	51.3
40	2.5	5	7.5	10	12.5	15	17.5	20	22.5	25	27.5	30	32.5	35	37.5	40	42.5	45	47.5	50

Number Correct

Number of Items

	21	22	23	24	25	26	27	28	29	30	31	32	33	34	35	36	37	38	39	40
1																				
2																				
3																				
4																				
5																				
6																				
7																				
8																				
9																				
10																				
11																				
12																				
13																				
14																				
15																				
16																				
17																				
18																				
19																				
20																				
21	100																			
22	95.4	100																		
23	91.3	95.6	100																	
24	87.5	91.6	95.8	100																
25	84	88	92	96	100															
26	80.8	84.6	88.5	92.3	96.2	100														
27	77.8	81.5	85.2	88.9	92.6	96.3	100													
28	75	78.6	82.1	85.7	89.3	92.9	96.4	100												
29	72.4	75.9	79.3	82.8	86.2	89.7	93.1	96.6	100											
30	70	73.3	76.7	80	83.3	86.7	90	93.3	96.7	100										
31	67.7	70.9	74.2	77.4	80.6	83.9	87.1	90.3	93.5	96.7	100									
32	65.6	68.8	71.9	75	78.1	81.2	84.4	87.5	90.6	93.8	96.9	100								
33	63.6	66.7	69.7	72.7	75.8	78.8	81.8	84.8	87.8	90.9	93.9	96.9	100							
34	61.8	64.7	67.6	70.6	73.5	76.5	79.3	82.4	85.3	88.2	91.2	94.1	97.1	100						
35	60	62.9	65.7	68.9	71.4	74.3	77.1	80	82.9	85.7	88.6	91.4	94.3	97.1	100					
36	58.3	61.1	63.8	66.7	69.4	72.2	75	77.8	80.6	85.7	86.1	88.9	91.7	94.9	97.2	100				
37	56.8	59.5	62.2	64.9	67.6	70.3	72.9	75.7	78.4	81.1	83.8	86.5	89.2	91.9	94.6	97.3	100			
38	55.3	57.9	60.5	63.2	65.8	68.4	71.2	73.7	76.3	78.9	81.6	84.2	86.8	89.5	92.1	94.7	97.3	100		
39	53.8	56.4	58.9	61.5	64.1	66.7	69.2	71.8	74.4	76.9	79.5	82.1	84.6	87.2	89.7	92.3	94.9	97.4	100	
40	52.5	55	57.5	60	62.5	65	67.5	70	72.5	75	77.5	80	82.5	85	87.5	90	92.5	95	97.5	100

Spelling Power

Lesson 1: Short Vowel Spellings

Word Bank

hamper	optimism	dispense	literal	criminal
impulsive	accomplice	mustache	valid	enhance

Key Concepts

1. Short vowel sounds are often spelled with single vowel letters.
   comic   bankrupt

2. Short vowel sounds include \a\ as in *hat*, \e\ as in *net*, \i\ as in *did*, \o\ as in *lot*, and \u\ as in *cup*.

Spelling Practice

Choose the word from the Word Bank defined by each phrase. Write your choices on the lines. Then circle the short vowel(s) that you hear in each word.

_____ **1.** hair on the upper lip

_____ **2.** helper in crime

_____ **3.** to hinder *or* a container for dirty clothes

_____ **4.** related to crime *or* person committing crimes

_____ **5.** habit of seeing the best in things

_____ **6.** acting without forethought

_____ **7.** to distribute

_____ **8.** to increase or improve

_____ **9.** logically sound, accurate, or effective

_____ **10.** according to dictionary definitions

LESSON 1 continued

Spelling in Context

Write the word from the Word Bank that best fits in each "Tom Swiftie" pun below. Use the Key Concepts to help you spell short vowel sounds correctly.

1. "This vending machine doesn't _____ apples or oranges," said Tom fruitlessly.

2. "I can wash all the clothes in my _____ now that I have a whole box of detergent," said Tom cheerfully.

3. "It's hard to feel _____ about Chicago's football team," said Tom bearishly.

4. "You caught me, Officer; I admit that I'm a(n) _____," said Tom crookedly.

5. "No one else is with me. My _____ has the day off," Tom continued helplessly.

Proofreading Practice

Read the paragraph. Find the five misspelled words and circle them. Then, on the numbered lines below, write the correct spelling for each circled word.

　　　Archaeologist Yuan Zhongyi made what seemed an impulsave decision in 1974. Assuming that a farmer's far-fetched claims were valed, Yuan started a dig in a remote Chinese field. Soon he had leteral proof that a two-thousand-year-old legend was true. He found a buried army of life-sized clay soldiers guarding the tomb of China's first emperor. Each soldier was unique, even down to the mustaiche. Yuan's work continues to anhance our knowledge of the ancient world.

1. _____   3. _____   5. _____

2. _____   4. _____

Spelling Application

Listed below are five additional words that follow the short-vowel patterns you have learned. Write each word on the line and circle the short vowel or vowels. Then on a separate piece of paper, create acrostics for the five words. For each acrostic, choose words or phrases reflecting the meaning of the spelling word. Check a dictionary if necessary. Look at the example to help you get started.

Example:　comics　　　　**c**olorful
　　　　　　　　　　　　outrageous
　　　　　　　　　　　　making us laugh
　　　　　　　　　　　　in the newspaper
　　　　　　　　　　　　creative
　　　　　　　　　　　　Sunday funnies

1. astronomical _____   4. fragment _____

2. budget _____   5. monstrosity _____

3. emphasis _____

Spelling Power

Lesson 2: Long Vowel Spellings

Word Bank

sustain	feasible	disagreeable	dehydrated	gyrate
overblown	encroach	mutually	butte	euphonium

Key Concepts

Long vowel sounds can be spelled with vowel combinations as well as with single vowels.

- The \ā\ sound can be spelled *ai, ay,* or *a_e.*
  st<u>ai</u>n   pl<u>ay</u>ful   gr<u>a</u>p<u>e</u>
- The \ē\ sound can be spelled *ea, ee, e, y,* or *e_e.*
  r<u>ea</u>ch   s<u>ee</u>k   d<u>e</u>cal
  melod<u>y</u>   comp<u>e</u>t<u>e</u>
- The \ī\ sound can be spelled *i, y,* or *i_e.*
  b<u>i</u>as   sk<u>y</u>   pr<u>i</u>z<u>e</u>

- The \ō\ sound can be spelled *oa, ow, o,* or *o_e.*
  r<u>oa</u>d   bl<u>ow</u>   als<u>o</u>   cl<u>o</u>s<u>e</u>
- The \ū\ sound can be spelled *ou, ew, eu, u, ue,* or *u_e.*
  c<u>ou</u>pon   f<u>ew</u>   f<u>eu</u>d   <u>u</u>sual
  T<u>u</u>esday   c<u>u</u>t<u>e</u>

Spelling Practice

Write the words from the Word Bank in alphabetical order. Circle the letters that spell the long vowel sound(s) in each word.

Example: _____att<u>ai</u>n_____

1. _____
2. _____
3. _____
4. _____
5. _____

6. _____
7. _____
8. _____
9. _____
10. _____

LESSON 2 continued

Spelling in Context

In each sentence, a word is missing. Write the correct word from the Word Bank on the line. Use the Key Concepts to help you spell the words correctly.

_____ **1.** After hiking for an hour in the desert, we began to feel _____.

_____ **2.** We watched a pair of hawks swoop and _____ in a cloudless sky.

_____ **3.** We cut across a sandy canyon, hoping not to _____ on private property.

_____ **4.** As a jackrabbit bounded off, we wondered where it found enough water to _____ life.

_____ **5.** Back at camp, we found the taste of cool lemonade far from _____.

Proofreading Practice

Read the paragraph. Find the five misspelled words and circle them. Then, on the numbered lines below, write the correct spelling for each circled word.

Were his dreams of climbing Mount McKinley just overblone fantasies? Climbing a bute might have challenged some people, but Erik Weihenmayer intended to go up the mountain. Although Weihenmayer had been blinded at thirteen, he was sure that the climb was fesible. Already an experienced climber, he began the ascent of McKinley with a party of sighted climbers. By mootually supporting one another, they succeeded. Weihenmayer became the first blind man ever to reach McKinley's 20,320-foot peak. He wished he could blow a uphonium to spread the news.

1. _____   **3.** _____   **5.** _____

2. _____   **4.** _____

Spelling Application

Below are five additional words that follow the long-vowel spelling patterns you have learned. Circle the letters that spell long-vowel sounds in these words. Then, using each word once, fill in the imaginary book titles.

futile   motivate   notable   ordeal   thrive

1. *Insects Can Help Your Garden* _____, by Leigh D. Bug

2. *How to* _____ *Yourself for Success,* by U. K. N. Dooit

3. *Lost in the Wilderness: My* _____, by Sir Vyval F. D. Fittess

4. _____ *Ideas That Brighten the Mind,* by N. Spur Ayshon

5. *Little-Known Feats and* _____ *Facts,* by Hooda Thunkitt

Spelling Power

Lesson 3: Double Consonants

Word Bank

eccentric	accommodate	vaccinate	exaggerate	recommend
questionnaire	appalling	apparently	embarrass	boycott

Key Concepts

1. Double consonants often follow short vowel sounds.

illness   motto

2. Double consonants usually represent a single unit of sound.

occupy   nagging

3. Sometimes double consonants represent two units of sound.

succeed (\k\ and \s\)

fishhook (\sh\ and \h\)

Spelling Practice

List the words from the Word Bank in alphabetical order. Circle the vowel or vowel pair that precedes each set of double consonants. If the double consonants represent one unit of sound, write *1*. If they represent two units of sound, write *2*.

Example: _____ accept, 2 _____

1. _____

2. _____

3. _____

4. _____

5. _____

6. _____

7. _____

8. _____

9. _____

10. _____

Spelling in Context

Decide which word from the Word Bank is defined by each phrase below. Write the word on the line. Refer to the Key Concepts to help you spell each word correctly.

_____ **1.** to refuse to buy, sell, or use a product

_____ **2.** written or printed series of questions

_____ **3.** to represent a thing as greater than it is

_____ **4.** causing horror; shocking; dreadful

_____ **5.** to have or make room for

LESSON 3 continued

Proofreading Practice

Read the paragraph. Find the five misspelled words and circle them. Then, on the numbered lines below, write the correct spelling for each circled word.

Exentric was a word often used to describe Lady Mary Wortley Montagu, a woman far ahead of her time. Born in 1689, Lady Mary was considered odd because of her brilliant mind. Did she embaras her husband, a government diplomat, by traveling with him to Turkey? Other Englishwomen of her era aparently disdained visiting that "heathen" land. Lady Mary found that Turkey had much to recomend it. There she learned how to vacinate children against smallpox, a practice that she later pioneered in England.

1. _____   4. _____

2. _____   5. _____

3. _____

Spelling Application

Listed below are eight additional words. Circle the double consonants in each. Write *1* after each word whose double consonants represent one unit of sound and *2* after each word whose double consonants represent two units of sound. Then use the words to fill in the crossword puzzle.

attend	attitude	dilemma	necessary
occasion	successor	warranty	withhold

Across
3. an important event
7. to keep something back
8. a promise of soundness or performance

Down
1. one who replaces someone else in office
2. a situation involving a difficult choice
4. to be present
5. needed or required
6. a state of mind or a feeling about something

Spelling Power

Lesson 4: Silent Consonants

Word Bank

debut	psychology	adjourn	acquaintance	mortgage
descend	subtle	acknowledgment	knoll	pneumonia

Key Concepts

1. Some silent consonants reflect earlier English pronunciations. In Middle English, the *k* in *knee* was sounded. Modern English drops the \k\ sound but keeps the spelling.

   acknowledgement   knoll

2. Some silent consonants reflect patterns of other languages. *Psychic* comes from Greek *psyche,* "soul." English speakers find \ps\ and \k\ hard to pronounce, so English drops the \p\ and \h\ sounds but keeps the spelling.

   psychology

3. Look for common letter combinations that include a silent letter. Some of these combinations include the following: *cq* (drop the \k\ sound); *pn* (drop the \p\ sound); *sc* (the letters sound a single \s\); *bt* (drop the \b\ sound).

   acquaintance   pneumonia   descend   subtle

4. Some words end with a silent letter. In *debut,* the *t* is not sounded.

   debut

5. Other words you should commit to memory.

   mortgage   adjourn

Spelling Practice

Choose the word from the Word Bank that comes from each source shown below. Write your choices on the lines. Circle the silent consonants in the words you write.

_____ 1. Greek *psyche,* "soul," + *logy,* "study"

_____ 2. Greek *pneumonia,* "lung disease," from *pneuma,* "wind, breath"

_____ 3. Old French *mort,* "death," + *gage,* "pledge"

_____ 4. Latin *de,* "down," + *scandere,* "to climb"

_____ 5. Old French *ad,* "to," + *jour,* "day"

_____ 6. Latin *subtilis,* "thin, fine"

_____ 7. Old English *cnoll,* "mound, small hill"

_____ 8. Old French *acointier,* "to familiarize"

_____ 9. Old English *ad,* "toward," + *cnawan,* "to know"

_____ 10. French *debuter,* "to make a first move in a game," from *de,* "away" + *but,* "goal"

LESSON 4 continued

Spelling in Context

Fill in each tongue twister with the word whose sound is shown. As you write the words, remember to include silent consonants.

1. Cynthia cycles to college \sī kol′ e jē\ _____ classes.

2. Why did mournful Morgan Jordan \môr′ gij\ _____ Mort George's morgue?

3. No \nōl\ _____ now known's so swiftly mown.

4. Would a judge \ə jurn′\ _____ a germy jury?

5. Moe noted numerous, new \nōō mōn′ yə\ _____ patients.

Proofreading Practice

Read the paragraph. Find the five misspelled words and circle them. Then, on the numbered lines below, write the correct spelling for each circled word.

If you know of Ben Franklin's strong aquaintance with music, you may wonder if he invented any musical instruments. Sure enough, in 1764 Franklin's "glass armonica" made its debeu. Its graduated glass bowls of water spun as a pedal was pumped. When players held their fingers to the glass rims, musical tones would rise or desend. The resulting melodies and chords were suttle and beautiful. Acnowledgement of Franklin's artistry came from Mozart, who composed two pieces for the glass armonica.

1. _____ 3. _____ 5. _____

2. _____ 4. _____

Spelling Application

Shown below are five additional words with silent consonant patterns that you have learned. Unscramble each set of letters to correctly spell the word it represents. Then circle the silent consonants in each word that you have written.

acquittal	ascending	pneumatic	psychiatrist	subtlety

1. telytubs   _____

2. claitutaq   _____

3. sattiphirscy   _____

4. gincandes   _____

5. cemutapin   _____

Spelling Power

Name _____ Date_____ Class _____

Spelling Power

Unit 1: Review Lessons 1–4

accommodate	acknowledgment	acquaintance	adjourn	appalling
descend	dispense	eccentric	enhance	exaggerate
feasible	hamper	impulsive	knoll	literal
questionnaire	mutually	valid	recommend	sustain

Fill in the word from the list above that best completes each sentence.

1. The hotel could not _____ any additional guests.

2. Alice waited for the machine to _____ soda.

3. Public television stations throughout the U.S. mailed a _____ to their viewers.

4. Candace would like some _____ for her hard work.

5. People who act in unique and unusual ways are often described as _____.

6. The teacher tells jokes to _____ her students' interest during long classes.

7. There is a sycamore tree growing on the _____.

8. Sometimes my spelling is _____.

9. Watching TV will not _____ your progress on your homework.

10. Walking from San Francisco to Paris is not _____.

For each phrase below, write the word from the list above that best fits the phrase.

acquaintance	hamper	exaggerate	descend	adjourn
optimism	impulsive	recommend	literal	mutually

11. tell a "fish story" _____

12. to hold back or a laundry basket _____

13. free-spirited _____

14. "Pleased to make your _____." _____

15. anticipating the best _____

16. "The court will now_____." _____

17. suggest, as at a restaurant _____

18. "They reached an agreement _____." _____

19. actual _____

20. opposite of ascend _____

Spelling Power   Grade 8   **9**

Spelling Power

Proofreading Application

Lessons 1–4
Read the following advice column. Find the twenty misspelled words and circle them. Then, on the numbered lines below, write the correct spelling for each circled word.

Dear Gabby,

My disagreable neighbor barges in and eats all my potato chips. When I ask him not to encroche on my property, he laughs and makes fun of my mustash. Should I shave it off?

Signed, Fuzzy Face

Dear Fuzzy,

Don't shave, don't be embarased, and don't be suttle with this crimenal nuisance. Lock your door and lock up the chips.

Dear Gabby,

My cable TV costs are so high that I'm going to have to morgage the house to pay them. Even with the cable, the TV works only if I gyrait the rabbit ears. Should I boycot the cable company?

Signed, Tube Troubles

Dear Troubles,

Your complaint sounds valed. This cable company aparently has overblone rates and underdone service. Quick—before the debu of the new fall shows—grab the Yellow Pages and find a better deal.

Dear Gabby,

I am six years old. My doctor and her acomplice gave my parents a questionaire about the shots I've had. Now they want to vacsinate me against all kinds of things. Save me!

Signed, Desperate

Dear Desperate,

Look at this situation with optomism. You don't want to get all dehidrated from the flu or get neumonia, do you? Ask your parents to use psycology. If they offer you a reward, you may not even notice the shots.

1. _____
2. _____
3. _____
4. _____
5. _____
6. _____
7. _____
8. _____
9. _____
10. _____

11. _____
12. _____
13. _____
14. _____
15. _____
16. _____
17. _____
18. _____
19. _____
20. _____

Name _____ Date_____ Class _____

Spelling Power

Lesson 5: Spelling the \ô\ Sound

Word Bank

falter	awkward	tawny	automation	fraudulent
thoughtlessness	distraught	haughty	discord	endorsed

Key Concepts

1. The \ô\ sound is spelled *au* or *aw* in most words.

   August   fault   awful   drawn

2. The \ô\ sound is spelled *a*, *augh*, or *ough* in some words.

   halt   daughter   ought

3. The \ôr\ sound is spelled *or* or *oar* in many words.

   form   coarse

Spelling Practice

Put the words from the Word Bank in alphabetical order. Circle the letters that spell the \ô\ or \ôr\ sound in each word.

1. _____   6. _____
2. _____   7. _____
3. _____   8. _____
4. _____   9. _____
5. _____   10. _____

Spelling in Context

Write the word from the Word Bank that fits in each "terse verse" rhyme. Refer to the Key Concepts to help you spell the words correctly.

Example: terrible breakfast treat: a __ __ __ l waffle   Answer: awful waffle

_____ 1. paid no attention to disharmony: ignored d __ __ __ __ __ d

_____ 2. dishonest purpose: f __ __ __ __ __ __ __ __ t intent

_____ 3. ungainly in reverse: a __ __ __ __ __ d backward

_____ 4. vain and scornful Dorothy: h __ __ __ __ __ y Dotty

_____ 5. mechanism to make sprinklers work by themselves: irrigation a __ __ __ __ __ __ __ __ n

Name _____ Date_____ Class _____

LESSON 5 continued

Proofreading Practice

Read the paragraph. Find the five misspelled words and circle them. Then, on the numbered lines below, write the correct spelling for each circled word.

What was killing the lions of Tanzania? As distroght rangers at Serengeti National Park watched helplessly, the tauwny cats ranging the savannah would mysteriously fawlter and die. Was their water supply polluted? Had the thotlessness of tourists introduced a deadly disease? The government quickly endoursed a study. Results were surprising: the lions had distemper, carried by local villagers' dogs. By inoculating dogs, rangers could save the lions.

1. _____   4. _____

2. _____   5. _____

3. _____

Spelling Application

Listed below are ten additional words that follow the patterns you have learned. Fill in each word next to its definition. Then circle the letters that spell the \ô\ or \ôr\ sound.

auditory   default   forethought   fraught   glorify
hydraulic   lawyer   remorse   tawdry   wrought

1. related to hearing   — — d — — — — y

2. to honor or praise   — — — — — f —

3. regret   r — — — — — e

4. attorney   — — — — — r

5. filled or laden   f — — — — — t

6. planned ahead   — — — e — — — — — — t

7. gaudy and cheap   — — — d — —

8. failure to perform or to pay   d — — — — l —

9. created or shaped   — r — — — — t

10. using water pressure   — y — — — — — i —

12 Grade 8

Spelling Power

Spelling Power

Lesson 6: Spelling the Schwa Sound \ə\

Word Bank

tangible	contemporary	perforate	admirable	manager
anonymous	inspector	superficial	colossal	saturate

Key Concepts

1. The schwa (ə) represents an indistinct vowel sound in unstressed syllables.

2. Any unstressed vowel may spell the \ə\ sound.
   <u>a</u>bove   it<u>e</u>m   ed<u>i</u>fy
   gall<u>o</u>n   cact<u>u</u>s

3. The \əl\ sound may be spelled *al, el, il, ol, ul,* or *le.*
   tri<u>al</u>   jew<u>el</u>   tendr<u>il</u>
   vi<u>ol</u>in   fear<u>ful</u>   app<u>le</u>

4. The \ər\ sound may be spelled *ar, er, ir, or, ur,* or *ure.*
   popul<u>ar</u>   cav<u>er</u>n   adm<u>ir</u>al
   doct<u>or</u>   s<u>ur</u>prise   fut<u>ure</u>

Spelling Practice

Choose the word from the Word Bank that fits each pronunciation. Write your choices on the lines. In the words you write, underline the letters that spell the sounds \ə\, \əl\, and \ər\.

Example: \sər prīz'\   ____surprise____

1. \in spek' tər\ _____
2. \kə los' əl\ _____
3. \soō' pər fish' əl\ _____
4. \ad' mər ə bəl\ _____
5. \sach' ə rāt'\ _____

6. \pûr' fə rāt'\ _____
7. \ə non' ə məs\ _____
8. \man' i jər\ _____
9. \kən tem' pə rer' ē\ _____
10. \tan' jə bəl\ _____

Spelling in Context

Write the word from the Word Bank that belongs with each group of terms. Use the Key Concepts to help you spell each word correctly.

_____ 1. pierce, drill, puncture

_____ 2. touchable, perceived through the senses, real

_____ 3. soak, fill to capacity, drench

_____ 4. examiner, reviewer, overseer

_____ 5. modern, current, of the same era

LESSON 6 continued

Proofreading Practice

Read the paragraph. Find the five misspelled words and circle them. Then, on the numbered lines below, write the correct spelling for each circled word.

Some people called him a colossle humbug. Others saw his plans as superficiel boasts. However, in June of 1859, the French acrobat Jean-François Gravelet turned his plans into reality: he walked a tightrope over Niagara Falls. The specially made rope, only three inches thick but more than 1,200 feet long, had been donated by an anonymus merchant. With admirabel calm, Gravelet balanced on the swaying line 180 feet above the chasm. He went on to repeat the feat weekly, at one point even carrying his managar along on his back.

1. _____   4. _____

2. _____   5. _____

3. _____

Spelling Application

Listed below are ten additional words that follow the patterns you have learned. Circle the letter(s) that spell the \ə\, \əl \, and \ər\ sounds.

astonish	bias	dilapidated	dismantle	personify
proposal	resolute	settle	tumult	urban

Fill in the correct word on each line. Be sure to spell the schwa sound correctly. Then draw lines to match the phrases in the two columns.

1. d_____ the statue   a. represent a president

2. u_____ comedian   b. worn corn

3. t_____ at sea   c. shock the doc

4. d_____ farm crop   d. ocean commotion

5. s_____ a tree   e. take apart art

6. overlook a b_____   f. determined German

7. p_____ a leader   g. calm a palm

8. doubt a p_____   h. miss a prejudice

9. r_____ citizen of Berlin   i. question a suggestion

10. a_____ the M.D.   j. town clown

Spelling Power

Lesson 7: The "Seed" Sound

Word Bank

exceedingly	succeeded	proceeding	procedure	receding
accede	antecedent	concede	intercede	supersedes

Key Concepts

1. The "seed" sound is spelled *cede* or *ceed* in most words:

pre<u>cede</u>   ex<u>ceed</u>

2. The "seed" sound is spelled *ced* in some words:

pre<u>ced</u>ing

3. The "seed" sound is spelled with an *s* for only one word family:

super<u>sede</u>   super<u>sed</u>ing

Spelling Practice

Put the words from the Word Bank in alphabetical order. Circle the letters that spell the "seed" sound. Then write the number of the Key Concept that applies to each word.

Example: _____ pre(ce)ding, 2 _____

1. _____   6. _____
2. _____   7. _____
3. _____   8. _____
4. _____   9. _____
5. _____   10. _____

Spelling in Context

For each sentence below, write the word from the Word Bank whose meaning is shown in parentheses. Use the Key Concepts to help you spell each word correctly.

_____ **1.** The two-year drought became the _____ (precursor) to a series of forest fires.

_____ **2.** The new right-turn law _____ (displaces) the old one as of next year.

_____ **3.** Josh was too young for civic orchestra tryouts, but his band teacher agreed to _____ (mediate) on his behalf.

_____ **4.** Rena's parents want her to skateboard only in protective gear, and she will _____ (agree) to their wishes.

_____ **5.** As the tide was _____ (going out), hundreds of sand dollars were revealed on the beach.

LESSON 7 continued

Proofreading Practice

Read the paragraph. Find the five misspelled words and circle them. Then, on the numbered lines below, write the correct spelling for each circled word.

What would you do if you saw an exceedingly bright, brand-new star in the sky? People saw just that when a supernova appeared in 1572, proseeding to shine until 1574. No one knew that this star was the dying explosion of a distant sun. Danish astronomer Tycho Brahe succeded in finding the "new" star's distance and position, even though the telescope had not yet been invented. His proceedure involved taking precise, hourly measurements over many months. Scientists then had to conceed that even stars might not be permanent fixtures in the sky.

1. _____   4. _____

2. _____   5. _____

3. _____

Spelling Application

Below are five additional words with patterns you have learned. Circle the letters that spell the "seed" sound.

cede   preceding   proceeds   succeeding   superseded

Use the grid to decode each word. The first digit in each number is that in the first horizontal row; the second, that in the first vertical column. (For example, 13-51-41 would be LED.) Then draw lines to match words and meanings.

	1	2	3	4	5
1	A	B	C	D	E
2	F	G	H	I,J	K
3	L	M	N	O	P
4	Q	R	S	T	U
5	V	W	X	Y	Z

1. 53-24-51-31-51-41-42-33-22
2. 34-54-31-31-51-51-41-42-33-22
3. 53-24-43-31-51-51-41-34
4. 34-54-53-51-24-34-51-41-51-41
5. 31-51-41-51

Words

1. _____

2. _____

3. _____

4. _____

5. _____

Meanings

a. displaced, outshone

b. previous

c. reaching a goal, following

d. relinquish

e. goes forward

Spelling Power

Lesson 8: Words with *ie* and *ei*

Word Bank

deceive	grievance	menagerie	premier	species
sovereignty	forfeiture	leisure	beige	feigned

Key Concepts

1. Follow the old rhyme for most *ie* and *ei* words with the \ē\ and \ā\ sounds:

Write *i* before *e* except after *c*,

shi<u>e</u>ld   bel<u>ie</u>f   rec<u>ei</u>ve

or when sounded as *a,* as in n<u>eig</u>hbor and w<u>eig</u>h.

2. Use *ei* to spell the \i\ sound in some words.

forf<u>ei</u>t   sover<u>ei</u>gn

3. Exceptions to memorize:

l<u>ei</u>sure   h<u>ei</u>r   spec<u>ie</u>s

n<u>ei</u>ther   w<u>ei</u>rd   prot<u>ei</u>n

Spelling Practice

Choose the word from the Word Bank that fits each meaning. Write your choices on the lines. Then write the number of the Key Concept that applies to each word.

_____ **1.** light tan

_____ **2.** to trick

_____ **3.** pretended

_____ **4.** surrendering something

_____ **5.** complaint

_____ **6.** free time

_____ **7.** wild animal exhibit

_____ **8.** most important

_____ **9.** independence or superiority

_____ **10.** type or kind

Spelling in Context

Write the word from the Word Bank whose sound is shown in each sentence below. Use the Key Concepts to spell each word correctly.

_____ **1.** American colonists had many a \grē′ vəns\ against England.

_____ **2.** King George refused to grant \sov′ rən tē\ to the colonies.

_____ **3.** To colonists, obeying laws made by a distant parliament represented a \fôr′ fi chər\ of rights.

_____ **4.** One of the colonists' \pri mēr′\ complaints was a law permitting homes to be searched at any time.

_____ **5.** Angry colonists might have thought, "A home is not a \mi naj′ ər ē\, to be visited by anyone who wishes!"

LESSON 8 continued

Proofreading Practice

Read the paragraph. Find the five misspelled words and circle them. Then, on the numbered lines below, write the correct spelling for each circled word.

Keeping absolutely still, a small, biege butterfly rests at liesure on a tree trunk. Its markings mimic the patterns of the bark, allowing it to decieve predators. Elsewhere a gray opossum lies limply curled as if unconscious. Its fiegned death fools attackers into leaving it alone. These examples show how protective adaptations aid individual animals, improving the chances that their speceis will survive.

1. _____   4. _____

2. _____   5. _____

3. _____

Spelling Application

Listed below are eight additional words that reflect the Key Concepts you have learned. After each word, write the number of the Key Concept that applies to the word.

achievement	conceited	counterfeit	heirloom
perceive	protein	unwieldy	veil

Use the words to complete the analogies below.

Example: leash : dog :: rein : _____horse_____

1. feat : _____ :: thankfulness : gratitude

2. speak : orate :: notice : _____

3. unclean : dirty :: _____ : awkward

4. _____ : face :: awning : window

5. carbohydrate : breads :: _____ : meats

6. genuine : _____ :: often : seldom

7. earn : salary :: inherit : _____

8. modern : antique :: modest : _____

Spelling Power

Unit 2: Review Lessons 5–8

anonymous	antecedent	colossal	contemporary	deceive
discord	endorsed	exceedingly	falter	feigned
fraudulent	haughty	leisure	menagerie	procedure
saturate	species	succeeded	supersedes	tangible

Use words from the list above to complete the following story. Write the correct word in each blank.

Juicy News from the Zoo

Late last Saturday, Inspector DeMarco received an _____ call. It seemed one of the animals in the zoo's

vast _____ had escaped. The animal, a _____ ape weighing in at over 400 pounds, had

_____ illness and managed to _____ the zookeeper. The _____ was not difficult to

carry out. All the ape had to do was _____ a sponge with warm water from its feeding dish and place

the warm sponge on its forehead to create a _____ difference in temperature.

The zoo's veterinarian was fooled by the ape's _____ behavior and she rushed to find some medicine

at an _____ fast pace, leaving the cage door open behind her. The clever ape did not _____

for an instant and slipped out of its cage. All of the other animals began to jump and screech, causing

_____. Inspector DeMarco reviewed the case at his _____. Finally, he expressed his opinion.

"An animal's need for food _____ all other needs," a view which the zookeeper _____ as well.

With that remark, Inspector DeMarco proceeded to walk down the street to Fruity Fran's Juice Bar, newly built to

satisfy the _____ fitness craze. There, in the juice bar, sat the ape, enjoying a banana smoothie. The

inspector had _____ in his quest. After being promised an occasional trip to the juice bar, the ape

agreed to go back to the zoo.

"When it comes to this particular _____ of animal," said the _____ inspector, with evident

pride, "there is only one proper _____ in the equation 'If Ape then Banana.'"

Spelling Power

Proofreading Application

Lessons 5–8
Read the following weekly crime report. Find the twenty misspelled words and circle them. Then, on the numbered lines below, write the correct spelling for each circled word.

East Park Distraut residents report odd behavior by an unknown speceis of bird. The large and akward avians, with tauny wings and green bodies, attack the umbrellas and steal the tuna sandwiches of locals spending liesure time at the park. People who try to interceed are pelted from the air with a rain of tuna, bread, and pickles. Police would like to question the managar of a traveling menegerie who hastily left the area earlier this year.

Midtown At the corner of Fifth and Market Streets, police briefly detained a speaker who was upbraiding passing pedestrians for their thotlessness. The speaker, taking breaks to use his cell phone and play a hand-held video game, claimed that otomation is erasing people's free will. He insisted that listeners give up their superficiel ways and acsede to his demand for the soveriegnty of a technology-free state.

Hillside Witnesses saw an irate customer use a plastic fork to perferate numerous balloons advertising a special at the Oak St. Beep-Beep Burger. The vandal, who wore plaid shorts and had a reseeding hairline, was last seen proceding eastward in a biege sedan. An inspecter praised witnesses' admerable speed at reporting the incident. Police consede that they have so far made no arrests.

1. _____
2. _____
3. _____
4. _____
5. _____
6. _____
7. _____
8. _____
9. _____
10. _____

11. _____
12. _____
13. _____
14. _____
15. _____
16. _____
17. _____
18. _____
19. _____
20. _____

Spelling Power

Lesson 9: Doubling the Final Consonant

Word Bank

controller	propellant	commitment	occurrence	dispelling
transmitter	deterred	regrettable	regretful	committed

Key Concepts

Double a word's final consonant to add a suffix if all four of the following conditions apply:

1. The word ends in a single consonant.
   repel + ent + repellent
   (compare: depend + ent = dependent)

2. A single vowel precedes the consonant.
   upset + ing = upsetting
   (compare: repeat + ing = repeating)

3. The word's last syllable is stressed.
   sub mit' + ed = submitted
   (compare: e' dit + ed = edited)

4. The suffix begins with a vowel.
   forget + able = forgettable
   (compare: forget + ful = forgetful)

Spelling Practice

Choose the word from the Word Bank made by combining each word root and suffix. Write the correct words on the lines.

1. occur + ence = _____

2. dispel + ing = _____

3. regret + able = _____

4. transmit + er = _____

5. deter + ed = _____

6. commit + ed = _____

7. control + er = _____

8. propel + ant = _____

9. regret + ful = _____

10. commit + ment = _____

Spelling in Context

Fill in the missing words from the Word Bank. Use the Key Concepts to spell each word correctly.

1. As _____ of the Science Club's treasury, Paul kept the books.

2. He had made a _____ to careful accounting.

3. Only one thing _____ him from balancing the budget.

4. He had overlooked a check for model rocket _____.

5. His error was _____ but understandable.

LESSON 9 continued

Proofreading Practice

Read the paragraph. Find the five misspelled words and circle them. Then, on the numbered lines below, write the correct spelling for each circled word.

Where in the solar system, beyond Earth, is the occurence of life most likely? It may be on Europa, one of Jupiter's moons. The spacecraft Galileo is dispeling the myth that these moons are barren rock. Images show that Europa has water, heat, and organic compounds–the essentials of life as we know it. Scientists are regrettful that Galileo can't reveal more, but its transmiter is damaged. Still NASA is commited to exploring Europa's mysteries–and its promise.

1. _____   4. _____

2. _____   5. _____

3. _____

Spelling Application

Below are five additional words that reflect the Key Concepts you have learned. Circle the word that has no double consonants. Then explain which of the four conditions this word does not meet.

excelling   forbidden   propeller   traveling   unforgettable

_____

_____

Choose the best word to complete each imaginary business address. Read each address carefully to find clues to the correct answer. Write your choices on the lines.

1. Happy _____
   Maps and Tour Books
   123 Gogh Way
   Waitfer, ME

2. Acme _____ Co.
   360 Spin Circle
   Aeronaut, TX

3. _____ with Electronics
   Computer Sales & Service
   500 Megahertz Drive
   Didgit, AL

4. _____ Fruit Produce
   Granny Smith, Mgr.
   80 Pippin Place
   Apple, CO

5. _____ Tunes
   Band and Music Supplies
   76 Trombones Square
   Oompah, PA

Spelling Power

Lesson 10: Dropping the Final Silent e

Word Bank

confidence	imposing	intriguing	legislator	menacing
senator	juicy	comparably	doubly	wholly

Key Concepts

1. To add a suffix starting with a vowel, drop a word's final silent e.

   debate + able = debatable

   urge + ent = urgent

   file + ing = filing

2. Drop the e to add -y.

   nose + y = nosy

3. To add -ly to most words ending in le, drop the le.

   able + ly = ably

4. Exceptions to memorize:

   mile + age = mileage

   whole + ly = wholly

   pale + ly = palely

Spelling Practice

Choose the word from Word Bank that combines each word root and suffix. Write your choice on the line. Then write the number of the Key Concept that applies to your choice.

Example: nose + y = ___nosy, 2___

1. legislate + or = _____
2. juice + y = _____
3. confide + ence = _____
4. intrigue + ing = _____
5. menace + ing = _____
6. whole + ly = _____
7. senate + or = _____
8. comparable + ly = _____
9. impose + ing = _____
10. double + ly = _____

Spelling in Context

Write the word from the Word Bank that fits in each sentence.

1. Our St. Bernard is _____ preoccupied with food.

2. He likes nothing better than a _____ steak.

LESSON 10 continued

3. Though he may look _____, he is still just a puppy.

4. He has a big appetite and a _____ big heart.

5. We think he looks dignified, so we named him _____ Sam.

Proofreading Practice

Read the paragraph. Find the five misspelled words and circle them. Then, on the numbered lines below, write the correct spelling for each circled word.

   Patrick Henry did not think himself an imposeing young man. His rural accent and his lack of money made him doubley self-conscious. However, he found the practice of law intrigueing, so he worked on his speaking skills until he gained confidance. Soon he was elected as a legislateor in the colony of Virginia. There his speeches electrified listeners. His famous words, "Give me liberty or give me death," have inspired generations of Americans.

1. _____   **3.** _____   **5.** _____

2. _____   **4.** _____

Spelling Application

Put together the word roots and suffixes below to form eight more words that follow the patterns you have learned. Use the Key Concepts to spell each word correctly. Then, to check your spelling, find and circle each word in the word ribbon.

1. ample + ly = _____

2. endure + able = _____

3. intervene + ing = _____

4. liberate + or = _____

5. enhance + ed = _____

6. provide + ent = _____

7. seclude + ed = _____

8. thrive + ing = _____

troliberatoriousinterveningapsecludedworenhancedsteamplythendurableakythrivingoneprovidentuche

Spelling Power

Lesson 11: Keeping the Final Silent e

Word Bank

endorsement	incitement	remorseful	remorseless	judgment
advantageous	replaceable	foreseeable	canoeist	decreeing

Key Concepts

1. To add a suffix starting with a consonant, keep a word's final silent e.

spite + ful = spiteful

place + ment = placement

2. Memorize two exceptions:

judge + ment = judgment

awe + ful = awful

3. To add a suffix starting with *a* or *o*, keep the e in words with the soft *c* or *g* sound.

trace + able = traceable

outrage + ous = outrageous

4. To add most suffixes to words ending in *ee* or *oe*, keep the final e.

free + dom = freedom

free + ing = freeing

hoe + ing = hoeing

Spelling Practice

Choose the word from the Word Bank that combines each word root and suffix. Write your choice on the line. Then write the number of the Key Concept that applies to your choice.

Example: free + dom = _____ freedom, 4 _____

1. advantage + ous = _____

2. canoe + ist = _____

3. decree + ing = _____

4. endorse + ment = _____

5. foresee + able = _____

6. judge + ment = _____

7. incite + ment = _____

8. replace + able = _____

9. remorse + ful = _____

10. remorse + less = _____

Spelling in Context

Write the word that best fits in each sentence. Use the Key Concepts to spell the words correctly.

1. By _____ taxes on basics such as tea, England's Parliament created hardships for American colonists.

2. King George's _____ of the taxes fueled colonists' anger.

LESSON 11 continued

3. The colonists' reaction to Parliament might have been _____, but apparently it was not.

4. Neither the king nor the members of Parliament seemed _____ when colonists protested.

5. This lack of concern was one more _____ to revolution.

Proofreading Practice

Read the paragraph. Find the five misspelled words and circle them. Then, on the numbered lines below, write the correct spelling for each circled word.

Could the old islander's claim be true? Could he really guide a canoist five hundred miles between two tiny atolls—using no navigation equipment at all? In the vast and remorsless Pacific, a small error could be fatal. Yet the judgement of Hipour, a traditional Micronesian navigator, proved accurate. His advantagous knowledge of currents, stars, and natural signs brought the canoe safely to its goal. His 1970 feat showed that traditional ways are not always easily replacable.

1. _____ **3.** _____ **5.** _____

2. _____ **4.** _____

Spelling Application

Here are six additional words that reflect the Key Concepts you have learned. Fill in the word that best completes each tongue twister.

| courageous | entirely | guaranteeing | manageable | purposeful | tiptoeing |

1. Tricia's _____ entrapped in truck tire trouble.

2. May my mammoth be _____, Ma'am.

3. The aged sage is _____.

4. Perfectly _____ persons pivot.

5. It's trim Tim Tripp _____.

6. Grand trees _____ teeming greenery grow.

Spelling Power

Lesson 12: The Final *y*

Word Bank

prepayment	defiant	verifiable	employer	jeopardize
anthologies	glorifying	essayist	novelties	clarifying

Key Concepts

When adding suffixes to words that end in *y*:

1. Change the *y* to *i* if a consonant precedes the *y*.
pry + ed = pried
fancy + ful = fanciful
rely + es = relies

2. Keep the *y* when adding *-ing*.
pry + ing = prying

3. Keep the *y* if a vowel precedes it.
play + ful = playful
joy + ous = joyous
relay + s = relays

Spelling Practice

Choose the word from the Word Bank that combines each word root and suffix. Write your choice on the line. Then write the number of the Key Concept that applies to your choice.

Example: rely + ance = _____ reliance, 1 _____

1. jeopardy + ize = _____

2. verify + able = _____

3. novelty + es = _____

4. anthology + es = _____

5. defy + ant = _____

6. glorify + ing = _____

7. clarify + ing = _____

8. essay + ist = _____

9. prepay + ment = _____

10. employ + er = _____

Spelling in Context

Write the word from the Word Bank that best fits in each sentence. Use the Key Concepts to spell the words correctly.

1. Mark Twain once wrote a humorous tale _____ a frog.

2. Twain seldom received _____ for his early work.

3. In Nevada, Twain's _____ was a newspaper editor.

4. Twain's _____ nature led him to criticize leading citizens.

5. His barbs did not _____ the newspaper's success.

LESSON 12 continued

Proofreading Practice

Read the paragraph. Find the five misspelled words and circle them. Then, on the numbered lines below, write the correct spelling for each circled word.

    If you love writing and reading essays—or even if you don't—you can thank Michel de Montaigne, the world's first essaist. Montaigne's brief prose pieces, each clarifing his thoughts on a single topic, were noveltys in his day. Some of his essays were based on verifyable facts; others were speculation. Montaigne died in 1592, but his works still appear in some anthologys.

1. _____ 4. _____

2. _____ 5. _____

3. _____

Spelling Application

Below are six more words that reflect the Key Concepts you have learned. First write the number of the Key Concept that applies to each word. Then fill in the words in the "Tom Swiftie" puns.

1. deployment   3. pettily   5. strategies

  _____ _____ _____

2. electrifying   4. pleasantries   6. undeniable

  _____ _____ _____

7. "My love of camping is _____," said Tom intently.

8. "This storm is _____!" said Tom currently.

9. "I have a dog, two cats, and a gerbil," said Tom _____.

10. "I've been exchanging _____ with my dad's dad," said Tom grandly and sunnily.

11. "Did you hear about the army's _____ in the combat zone?" asked Tom warily.

12. "Here are my _____ for getting that player out of the basketball game," said Tom foully.

Spelling Power

Unit 3: Review Lessons 9–12

advantageous	anthologies	clarifying	commitment	comparably
confidence	controlling	decreeing	defiant	deterred
essayist	imposing	judgment	intriguing	legislator
occurrence	regretful	remorseful	replaceable	verifiable

Use the word roots listed above to create words that complete the following sentences. Write the words in the blanks.

1. Playing a professional sport requires _____ and dedication.

2. Martha's excellent test scores give her _____.

3. After sneaking into the kitchen and eating his sister's birthday cake, Mike felt _____.

4. Many people find mystery novels _____.

5. The antique china that Ellen broke was not _____.

6. When police checked the facts, they learned that the suspect's alibi was not _____.

7. Although both cars were expensive, they were _____ priced.

8. The _____ handed down by the jury surprised the lawyers.

9. Some pets may find their bossy owners too _____.

10. The grand crystal chandelier was quite _____.

11. Kate felt _____ that she had to leave the party so early.

12. If you read those _____, you may find the story you are looking for.

13. Christopher fell asleep while the teacher was _____ her point.

14. Stephen will not be _____ by challenges.

15. Since Jane became a state representative, she has proven herself a talented _____.

16. Candace is very stubborn and sometimes _____.

17. The fire in the nearby forest was an unfortunate _____.

18. In medieval times, nothing would stop a king from _____ banishment for debtors.

19. Jonathan Swift, who wrote *A Modest Proposal,* was a wonderful _____.

20. Knowing more than one language is _____ when traveling.

Spelling Power

Proofreading Application

Lessons 9–12

Read the following letters from camp. Find the twenty misspelled words and circle them. Then, on the numbered lines below, write the correct spelling for each circled word.

Dear Mom and Dad,

Well, here I am at Camp Wackawacka. There is no foreseable way that I won't have fun, so don't worry that your prepaiment was wasted. The hamburgers are juicey and the lake is beautiful. I'm commited to becoming an expert canooist. I'll bring you some noveltys from the camp store.

Love, Your Happy Kid

Dear Mom and Dad,

Everything's still great except for one regretable incident. Do you remember that Senater Vail was coming to give the camp her endorsment? She arrived the day I tested a model speedboat fueled with my own homemade propelant. I didn't mean to jeopordize our reputation, but as the camp counselors put it, soaking a government official is not the best way of glorifiying our camp.

Love, Your Red-Faced Kid

Dear Mom and Dad,

Don't trust the counselors' judgement! I'm dispeling any false ideas they've given you about me. It's wholely untrue that I built a model transmiter to order pizza. I didn't broadcast those menaceing sounds on ghost-story night either. The counselors are doubley strict with me. They even want me to do chores—do they think the camp director is my emploier?? They're remorsless! When can I come home?

Love, Your Misunderstood Kid

1. _____

2. _____

3. _____

4. _____

5. _____

6. _____

7. _____

8. _____

9. _____

10. _____

11. _____

12. _____

13. _____

14. _____

15. _____

16. _____

17. _____

18. _____

19. _____

20. _____

Spelling Power

Lesson 13: The Suffixes *-ise*, *-ize*, and *-yze*

Word Bank

improvise	monopolize	paralyze	televise	categorize
enterprise	apologize	scrutinize	emphasize	compromise

Key Concepts

1. The ending \īz\ is spelled *-ize* in many words.
itemize   realize

2. The ending \īz\ is spelled *-ise* in some words.
surprise   demise

3. The ending \īz\ is spelled *-yze* in only a few words.
analyze

Spelling Practice

Put the words from the Word Bank in alphabetical order. In each word, circle the letters that spell the \īz\ ending.

Example: analyze

1. _____   **6.** _____

2. _____   **7.** _____

3. _____   **8.** _____

4. _____   **9.** _____

5. _____   **10.** _____

Spelling in Context

Write the word from the Word Bank that best fits in each sentence. Be sure to spell the \īz\ sound correctly.

1. Rod showed great _____ in auditioning for concert band.

2. He knew that the director would _____ his technique.

3. Rod planned to play a Mozart piece and then _____ some jazz.

4. He hoped that nervousness would not _____ him.

5. If he made a mistake, Rob wondered whether he should stop and _____ or continue.

LESSON 13 continued

Proofreading Practice

Read the paragraph. Find the five misspelled words and circle them. Then, on the numbered lines below, write the correct spelling for each circled word.

Famed trumpeter Wynton Marsalis is not easy to categorise. He likes to emphasise links between classical music and jazz. His parents did not compromize his musical education, teaching him both forms. Besides playing and composing, Marsalis works to open the world of music to young people. In the 1990s, a national network contracted to televize his series "Marsalis on Music." He hopes not to monopolyze the spotlight, but to create space for developing musicians.

1. _____   4. _____

2. _____   5. _____

3. _____

Spelling Application

Below are eight additional words that reflect the Key Concepts you have learned. Match each word to its origins.

authorize	harmonize	pulverize	sympathize
chastise	despise	franchise	hydrolyze

1. Latin *pulvis,* "dust"   _____

2. Greek *harmos,* "shoulder; joint"   _____

3. Old French *franche,* "free"   _____

4. Latin *castigare,* "to punish"   _____

5. Greek *hydro,* "water," + *lysis,* "dissolve"   _____

6. Latin *auctor,* "creator"   _____

7. Greek *syn,* "like," + *pathos,* "emotion"   _____

8. Latin *de,* "down," + *specere,* "to look"   _____

Spelling Power

Lesson 14: The Suffixes *-ary* and *-ory*

Word Bank

sensory	satisfactory	customary	mandatory	literary
revolutionary	elementary	introductory	complementary	exploratory

Key Concepts

The suffixes *-ary* and *-ory* often form adjectives.

1. The suffix *-ary* may be pronounced \er' ē\ or \ər ē'\.

   imaginary   binary

2. The suffix *-ory* may be pronounced \ôr' ē\ or \ər ē'\.

   oratory   advisory

Spelling Practice

Write the words from the Word Bank in alphabetical order. Circle the *-ary* or *-ory* suffix in each word.

Example: _____ binary _____

1. _____
2. _____
3. _____
4. _____
5. _____

6. _____
7. _____
8. _____
9. _____
10. _____

Spelling in Context

Write the word from the Word Bank that best fits in each sentence. Be sure to spell the words correctly.

1. Was that your grandfather I saw at the _____ school?

2. Yes, he teaches _____ poetry writing in the afternoons.

3. It's an _____ course for anyone who's interested.

4. He shows people how to create striking _____ images.

5. Most people think their writing is barely _____, but my grandfather helps them see their strengths.

LESSON 14 continued

Proofreading Practice

Read the paragraph. Find the five misspelled words and circle them. Then, on the numbered lines below, write the correct spelling for each circled word.

Helen Cordero didn't realize how revolutionery her idea was. A Native American potter, she decided to sculpt a figure of her grandfather telling tales, as was customery in her family. She painted the sculpture in complementry earth tones, using natural materials from her home area of Cochiti Pueblo, New Mexico. Soon her storyteller figures became mandatary items for collectors. Today her legacy preserves the Pueblo artistic and literery heritage.

1. _____   4. _____

2. _____   5. _____

3. _____

Spelling Application

Below are five more words that follow the patterns you have learned.

compulsory   exemplary   hereditary   primary   transitory

Write each word vertically. Then create an acrostic for each word. The terms in your acrostic should all relate to the word's meaning. Hint: You may use a dictionary if necessary.

Example:
b ase-2 number system
i nteresting
n o more than two different digits
a lot of ones and zeros
r epetitive
y our computer uses it

Spelling Power

Lesson 15: The Suffix *-ion*

Word Bank

provision	possession	deduction	aspiration	omission
erosion	diction	revelation	occupation	secession

Key Concepts

1. The suffix *-ion,* meaning "act of" or "state of," forms nouns.

2. Added to a word root, *-ion* becomes *-tion* or *-sion.* These syllables may be pronounced \shən\ or \zhən\.

   relation   equation
   tension   decision

3. Many word roots change form when *-tion* or *-sion* is added.

   assume + -ion = assumption

Spelling Practice

Choose the word from the Word Bank that is made from each word root. Write your choices on the lines.

1. possess _____
2. aspire _____
3. deduce _____
4. reveal _____
5. provide _____

6. secede _____
7. dict _____
8. occupy _____
9. erode _____
10. omit _____

Spelling in Context

Fill in the word from the Word Bank that best completes each sentence. Be sure to spell the \shn\ or \zhn\ sound correctly.

1. What lay behind the Confederacy's _____ from the Union?

2. Confederate leaders cited a gradual _____ of states' rights.

3. In ringing _____, Southern orators expressed a dread of an overly powerful central government.

4. The main _____ of many Southern leaders was proclaiming self-government.

5. Their _____ was not to destroy the Union, but to retain as much local control over their government as possible.

Name _____ Date_____ Class _____

Proofreading Practice

Read the paragraph. Find the five misspelled words and circle them. Then, on the numbered lines below, write the correct spelling for each circled word.

Seven young men in Texas called the police on March 22, 1998, with an amazing revelation. They had in their possetion a meteorite that had landed near their basketball court, and the meteorite was still warm. NASA scientists in Houston hurriedly made provition to examine the space rock. Their astonishing deductsion: the rock contained briny water 4.5 billion years old. The omition of just a few minutes' haste on the young men's part would have let the tiny droplets evaporate.

1. _____   3. _____   5. _____

2. _____   4. _____

Spelling Application

Below are five more words that follow the patterns you have learned. Choose the best word to fill in each imaginary book title. Hint: Carefully read the name of each book's author.

admission   accommodations   calculation   exertion   petition

1. *When the Cost of Vacation* _____ *Will Drop*, by Wendy Cowscomehome

2. *Learning Mental* _____, by Matt Matticks

3. *No* _____, by Doris Lockett

4. *Recovering from Strenuous* _____, by Mr. Lane Down

5. _____ *Your Representatives*, by Noah Vail

Spelling Power

Lesson 16: The Suffix -ous

Word Bank

harmonious	pious	miscellaneous	boisterous	valorous
fictitious	ingenious	gracious	contagious	hilarious

Key Concepts

The suffix -ous indicates an adjective.

1. Some adjectives ending in -ous do not have familiar word roots.

   jealous   tremendous   obvious

   serious   conscious   precious

2. Some word roots change form when -ous is added.

   vice + ous = vicious

   courtesy + ous = courteous

   religion + ous = religious

   disaster + ous = disastrous

Spelling Practice

Choose the adjective from the Word Bank based on each noun. Write your choices on the lines below.

1. valor: _____

2. grace: _____

3. harmony: _____

4. miscellany: _____

5. piety: _____

6. hilarity: _____

7. contagion: _____

8. fiction: _____

Write the two Word Bank adjectives that do not have familiar word roots.

9. _____

10. _____

Spelling in Context

For each set of adjectives, choose the word from the Word Bank whose meaning is similar. Write your choices on the lines below.

_____ 1. funny, humorous, amusing

_____ 2. catching, communicable, infectious

_____ 3. untrue, falsified, fabricated

_____ 4. devout, reverent, religious

_____ 5. pleasant, compatible, melodic

LESSON 16 continued

Proofreading Practice

Read the paragraph. Find the five misspelled words and circle them. Then, on the numbered lines below, write the correct spelling for each circled word.

At eighty-two, Thomas Jefferson was gracius enough to sit for sculptor John Henri Isaac Browere. The artist had an ingeneous plan for creating an exact likeness. He made a mold by covering Jefferson's face with plaster, inserting straws for breathing. Unfortunately, the plaster stuck. The valorus Jefferson stayed calm as Browere frantically worked with chisel, mallet, and other miscellaneus tools. Jefferson's boistrous seven-year-old grandson, however, shouted to the household that Jefferson was being attacked.

1. _____   4. _____

2. _____   5. _____

3. _____

Spelling Application

Listed below are six additional words reflecting the Key Concepts you have learned. Use the words to complete the verse below. Hint: Each pair of lines, beginning with (1) and (2), rhymes.

atrocious   ferocious   laborious   spacious   tenacious   uproarious

To a Neighbor

Sir, your dog is quite (1) _____

And its manners are (2) _____,

For at digging it's (3) _____

Even though its yard is (4) _____,

And its bark is so (5) _____

Living near has grown (6) _____.

Please do everyone a favor:

Train the creature!

Signed, Your Neighbor

Spelling Power

Unit 4: Review Lessons 13–16

aspiration	boisterous	categorize	compromise	customary
deduction	emphasize	erosion	harmonious	improvise
ingenious	mandatory	omission	paralyze	pious
revelation	revolutionary	satisfactory	sensory	valorous

Write the word from the list above that best fits each meaning.

1. reasonable conclusion _____
2. relating to the senses _____
3. something left out _____
4. brave _____
5. reach an agreement _____
6. put in order by group _____
7. act of wearing away _____
8. very clever _____
9. loud and spirited _____
10. something disclosed _____
11. devout _____
12. necessary, unavoidable _____
13. hope _____
14. to do with no preparation _____
15. to stop from moving _____

Write five sentences using the remaining spelling words from the word list above.

16. _____
17. _____
18. _____
19. _____
20. _____

Spelling Power

Proofreading Application

Lessons 13–16
Read the following summer book list. Find the twenty misspelled words and circle them. Then, on the numbered lines below, write the correct spelling for each circled word. Hint: Carefully read the names of each author.

Summer Reading List
1. Avoiding Contagios Diseases, by Steth O'Scope
2. Don't Apologise, by Stu Badd
3. The Truth About the South's Secetion, by Jess D. Facks
4. Miscellanius Details, by Ed Settera
5. The Risks of Free Enterprize, by Willy Makeitt
6. Introductery Fractions, by Delores Commen de Nommenator
7. Fictitius Excuses for All Occasions, by Liza Likearug
8. The Perils of Exploratary Surgery, by Dr. Sawyer Toeoff
9. The Graceious Host and Hostess, by T. N. Crumpetts
10. Possesion by Fear, by Freida D. Dark
11. Occupasion: Carpenter, by Sandy Boardz
12. Provition for Chance Events, by Lill Bittoluck
13. Complementory Foods, by Hammond Swiss
14. Proper Dicton or None at All, by Xavier Breath
15. Elementery Money Management, by Zelda Heirlooms
16. Why Televize Reruns? by Ben Dare and Don Datt
17. Hilarius Old Cartoons, by Felix Dakatt
18. Don't Monopolise the Conversation, by I. M. Perry Mount
19. Scrutinyze the Sky, by Seymour Starz
20. Literery Masterpieces, by Ed de Torreal

1. _____   11. _____

2. _____   12. _____

3. _____   13. _____

4. _____   14. _____

5. _____   15. _____

6. _____   16. _____

7. _____   17. _____

8. _____   18. _____

9. _____   19. _____

10. _____   20. _____

Spelling Power

Lesson 17: The Suffixes *-ible* and *-able*

Word Bank

indelible	intelligible	accessible	inflexible	eligible
charitable	durable	hospitable	inevitable	invariable

Key Concepts

1. The suffixes *-able* and *-ible* form adjectives.
   honorable   contemptible

2. Many word roots change when *-able* or *-ible* is added.
   rely + able = reliable
   admit + ible = admissible

3. Some adjectives ending in *-able* or *-ible* have Latin, rather than English, word roots.
   possible   portable

Spelling Practice

Choose the word from the Word Bank that best fits each meaning. Write your choices on the lines.

_____ 1. unchanging

_____ 2. kind; generous

_____ 3. understandable

_____ 4. warmly welcoming

_____ 5. unbending

_____ 6. easy to reach

_____ 7. hard to erase

_____ 8. not avoidable

_____ 9. sturdy; lasting

_____ 10. qualified; worthy

Spelling in Context

Write the *-able* or *-ible* adjective from the Word Bank that is related to each Latin word root and set of English words.

_____ 1. *caritas,* "love": cherish, charity, uncharitably

_____ 2. *eligere,* "to choose": elect, election, eligibility

_____ 3. *hospes,* "guest" or "host": hospice, hospital, hospitality

_____ 4. *intelligere,* "to perceive": intellect, intelligent, intelligence

_____ 5. *flexus,* "bent": reflex, flex, inflexibility

Name _____ Date _____ Class _____

Proofreading Practice

Read the paragraph. Find the five misspelled words and circle them. Then, on the numbered lines below, write the correct spelling for each circled word.

Several times a year, fantastic sky shows are accessable to everyone on the planet. Meteor showers are free—and fantastic. Their invarible timing reflects the earth's regular passage through the tails of comets orbiting the sun. Scan the sky after midnight on August 12, for instance, and it's inevitible that you'll see meteors. You won't need a telescope—just get a durible lawn chair, lean back, and look up. During a strong shower, nearly seventy shooting stars per hour will leave their indeleble impression on your mind.

1. _____   4. _____

2. _____   5. _____

3. _____

Spelling Application

Listed below are ten more words that follow the patterns you have learned. Unscramble each set of letters. Then write the words correctly.

agreeable   disposable   incomparable   interchangeable   knowledgeable
liable   peaceable   permissible   probable   responsible

_____ **1.** abiell

_____ **2.** rablebop

_____ **3.** bleareage

_____ **4.** bapeelace

_____ **5.** plebadossi

_____ **6.** ripemeslibs

_____ **7.** slonbeepirs

_____ **8.** crabalemonip

_____ **9.** ankledogbelew

_____ **10.** beachiglannneret

Name _____ Date _____ Class _____

Spelling Power

Lesson 18: Adding Prefixes

Word Bank

adjoined	misdeed	evacuate	misspelling	disappearance
adept	extensive	intolerance	insolvable	emigrate

Key Concepts

1. Prefixes change the meanings of word roots.
   ad- = toward
   dis- = not
   ex- (e-) = out, forth
   in- = into, not
   mis- = wrong, bad

2. Keep all the letters of a word root when you add a prefix.
   ad + just = adjust
   dis + agree = disagree
   dis + satisfy = dissatisfy
   mis + step = misstep
   mis + trust = mistrust

Spelling Practice

Choose the word from the Word Bank that best fits each definition. Write your choices on the lines.

_____ 1. wrong spelling

_____ 2. lack of tolerance

_____ 3. to empty out; to vacate

_____ 4. vanishing

_____ 5. not possible to solve

_____ 6. wrong action

_____ 7. was joined to

_____ 8. to move out of one's country

_____ 9. skilled

_____ 10. vast

Spelling in Context

Write the word from the Word Bank that completes each sentence. Use the Key Concepts to help you spell each word correctly.

1. On our trip, my hotel room _____ my parents' room.

2. We had to _____ the building when a fire alarm rang.

3. Later police were alerted to the _____ of a guest's jewelry.

4. A ransom note added suspense to the _____.

5. Detectives remarked on the _____ of several words in the note.

LESSON 18 continued

Proofreading Practice

Read the paragraph. Find the five misspelled words and circle them. Then, on the numbered lines below, write the correct spelling for each circled word.

Nikola Tesla (1856–1943) was an addept inventor. He launched his exttensive career when he was nine, creating an eggbeater powered by June bugs. As a young electrical engineer, he decided to emmigrate from Croatia to America. He worked for a time with Thomas Edison, despite Edison's inntolerance of his "ridiculous" ideas. By the late nineteenth century, Tesla had perfected alternating current, remote control, and the high-frequency generator called the Tesla coil. For Nikola Tesla, no electrical problem was innsolvable.

1. _____   4. _____

2. _____   5. _____

3. _____

Spelling Application

Listed below are eight more words that reflect the Key Concepts you have learned. Circle the prefix added to each word root.

adjacent   advent   disappoint   distraction
emit   infuriate   ineffective   misjudge

Write the words from the list to complete the "terse verse" rhymes.

1. _____ a scream = send out a shout

2. _____ doe = near deer

3. _____ the wise one = outrage the sage

4. _____ the city = let down the town

5. field trip _____ = excursion diversion

6. useless order = _____ directive

7. underestimate the chocolate = _____ the fudge

8. arrival of the concrete = cement _____

Spelling Power

Lesson 19: Assimilated Prefixes

Word Bank

irrational	assumption	immense	affirm	attested
accountant	illogical	immigrate	approval	aggressive

Key Concepts

Some prefixes may be assimilated, that is, they are partially absorbed into the word roots to make pronunciation easier.

1. Assimilated prefixes often result in double consonants.

   ad + fair = affair

2. The assimilated prefix *in-* (into, not) may be spelled *il-, im-,* or *ir-*:

   illegal   impress   irregular

3. The assimilated prefix *ad-* (to, toward) may be spelled *ac-, af-, ag-, al-, an-, ap-, as-,* or *at-*:

   account   affix   aggrandize
   allure   annotate   appoint
   assort   attune

Spelling Practice

Choose the words from the Word Bank that combine the root words and affixes shown. Write your choices on the lines.

Example: _aggrandize_   ad + grand + ize

_____ **1.** in + migrate   _____ **6.** ad + firm

_____ **2.** ad + count + ant   _____ **7.** in + mense

_____ **3.** in + logical   _____ **8.** ad + gress + ive

_____ **4.** ad + tested   _____ **9.** ad + prove + al

_____ **5.** in + rational   _____ **10.** ad + sume + tion

Spelling in Context

Write the correct word from the Word Bank to complete each analogy. Use the Key Concepts to help you spell assimilated prefixes correctly.

1. reveal : revelation :: assume : _____

2. logical : _____ :: pleasant : unpleasant

3. _____ : immigrant :: apply : applicant

4. disapproval : criticize :: _____ : compliment

5. art : designer :: math : _____

LESSON 19 continued

Proofreading Practice

Read the paragraph. Find the five misspelled words and circle them. Then, on the numbered lines below, write the correct spelling for each circled word.

In 1957, a small group of Arkansas teenagers took an imense step. These nine young people challenged the irational practice of racial segregation in public schools. As the first black students at Little Rock's all-white Central High School, they braved agressive protesters who hurled stones as well as insults. The nine students' persistence atested to their courage. Their success served to afirm the strength of the civil rights movement.

1. _____   4. _____

2. _____   5. _____

3. _____

Spelling Application

Listed below are eight more words that reflect the Key Concepts you have learned. Write each word next to its meaning and Latin origin.

allude   announce   assimilate   attracted
illiterate   imply   irreverence   irrigate

_____ **1.** unable to read: *in* (not) + *literae,* "letters"

_____ **2.** drawn toward: *ad* + *tractus,* "pulled"

_____ **3.** to blend in: *ad* + *similis,* "alike"

_____ **4.** to suggest: *in* (in) + *plicare,* "to fold"

_____ **5.** to make a sly or indirect reference: *ad* + *ludus,* "game; joke"

_____ **6.** to state publicly: *ad* + *nuntius,* "messenger"

_____ **7.** to bring water into a dry area: *in* (in) + *rigare,* "to water"

_____ **8.** disrespect: *in* (not) + *reverens,* "respecting"

Spelling Power

Lesson 20: The Prefixes *sub-* and *super-*

Word Bank

substantial	superlative	summon	superficially	sufficient
succumb	suspended	supplicant	survey	surmount

Key Concepts

1. The Latin prefix *sub-* means "under" or "from beneath."

subculture   subzero

2. The prefix *sub-* may be assimilated as *suc-, suf-, sum-, sup-,* or *sus-*.

suffix   suppress

3. The Latin prefix *super-* means "above" or "over."

superhuman   superstructure

4. The prefix *sur-* is another form of *super-*.

surcharge   surface   surpass

Spelling Practice

Choose the word from the Word Bank that fits each etymology (word origin) and meaning. Write your choices on the lines.

Example: ___surface___   outer part; top (*sur + facies,* "face")

_____ **1.** to give in (*sub + cumbere,* "to lie down")

_____ **2.** shallowly; on the surface (*super + facies,* "face")

_____ **3.** best; highest (*super + latus,* "carried")

_____ **4.** to overcome (*sur + mount*)

_____ **5.** postponed; dangling (*sub + pendere,* "to hang")

_____ **6.** one who pleads (*sub + plicare,* "to bend")

_____ **7.** to send for (*sub + monere,* "to warn")

_____ **8.** important; of value (*sub + stans,* "standing")

_____ **9.** enough (*sub + facere,* "to do")

_____ **10.** to look over (*sur + videre,* "to look")

LESSON 20 continued

Spelling in Context

Write the word from the Word Bank that best fits in each sentence. Use the Key Concepts to help you spell the words correctly.

_____ **1.** The young Confederate soldier was captured on a _____ mission near Vicksburg.

_____ **2.** A bayonet had wounded him _____.

_____ **3.** He tried to _____ up courage and dignity.

_____ **4.** He would not behave as a _____ before the enemy.

_____ **5.** His trial was _____ until officers could arrive.

Proofreading Practice

Read the paragraph. Find the five misspelled words and circle them. Then, on the numbered lines below, write the correct spelling for each circled word.

More than 2,500 years ago, the Maya had a sibstantial civilization in Mesoamerica. Supurlative farmers, architects, artists, and astronomers, they were able to sirmount many obstacles. Their complex writing system was suficient to create detailed records. Yet, mysteriously, they deserted their cities long before Europeans set foot in the New World. Did the Maya sucumb to drought, to infighting, or to a mighty enemy? No one knows.

1. _____ **3.** _____ **5.** _____

2. _____ **4.** _____

Spelling Application

Listed below are five more words that reflect the Key Concepts you have learned. Fill in the correct words from the list to complete the "Tom Swiftie" puns.

submit   suffocate   supplant   supplement   surrender

1. "I've forced several opponents to _____," said Tom winsomely.

2. "These animals must _____ to confinement," said Tom cagily.

3. "Hockey could _____ baseball as our national pastime," said Tom puckishly.

4. "This vitamin _____ comes only in bottles," said Tom uncannily.

5. "Open the air ducts before we _____," said Tom inventively.

Spelling Power

Unit 5: Review Lessons 17–20

accessible	adjoin	affirm	aggressive	approval
disappearance	durable	extensive	illogical	inevitable
intelligible	intolerance	invariable	irrational	misdeed
substantial	superficially	superlative	supplicant	surmount

Write the words from the list above whose prefixes have the meaning shown.

over; above (*super; sur*)   under; from beneath (*sub; sup*)

1. _____   4. _____

2. _____   5. _____

3. _____

Write the word that includes each prefix shown.

6. dis- _____   9. ex- _____

7. mis- _____   10. in- _____

8. ad- _____

Use the remaining words from the word list to write five sentences of your own.

11. _____

12. _____

13. _____

14. _____

15. _____

Spelling Power

Proofreading Application

Lessons 17–20

Read the following television listings. Find the twenty misspelled words and circle them. Then, on the numbered lines below, write the correct spelling for each circled word.

Monday Morning

9:00 *As the Planet Spins* – Pam meets a handsome and eligable acountant. Will she sucumb to his numerous charms? Meanwhile Arthur coldly makes the assumsion that Hugh would like to emmigrate to Siberia.

9:30 *Entertaining with Emily* – Tips for the hospitible hostess: making sure you have suffisient refreshments; how to loosen up inflexable guests; the correct way to submon a butler.

10:00 *The Sampsons* (rerun) – Midge, Helmer, Bert, and Visa fill out a surrvey and win a trip to Japan. While there, they develop a taste for sushi and decide to imagrate. With emense fanfare, Mr. Barns places himself in susspended animation.

10:30 *Mr. Fixer-Upper* – Becoming addept at removing stains and tackling other seemingly unsolvible laundry problems: instructions for removing indellable ink. Also, toxic fumes: knowing when to evvacuate.

11:00 *Celebrity Telethon* – Charitible benefit for those suffering from grammar phobia, chronic mispelling, or compulsive comma avoidance. Self-help strategies atested to by guest celebrities.

1. _____
2. _____
3. _____
4. _____
5. _____
6. _____
7. _____
8. _____
9. _____
10. _____
11. _____
12. _____
13. _____
14. _____
15. _____
16. _____
17. _____
18. _____
19. _____
20. _____

Spelling Power

Lesson 21: The Latin Word Roots *duc* and *port*

Word Bank

conductor	deduct	induce	productive	reducible
subdue	comport	transportation	supportive	portable

Key Concepts

1. The Latin word root *duc/duct* means "to lead."
   educate: to teach (lead forth)
   conduct: to direct (lead together)

2. The Latin word root *port* means "to carry" or "to bring."
   porter: one who carries
   import: to bring in goods
   report: to bring back news

Spelling Practice

Choose the word from the Word Bank that has each meaning and combination of word roots and affixes. Write your choices on the lines.

Example: ____educate____ *e + duc + ate* (to teach)

_____ **1.** *de + duct* (to remove or subtract)

_____ **2.** *con + duct + or* (director)

_____ **3.** *port + able* (easy to carry)

_____ **4.** *re + duc + ible* (capable of being made smaller)

_____ **5.** *pro + duct + ive* (yielding abundantly; accomplishing a great deal)

_____ **6.** *com + port* (to behave oneself)

_____ **7.** *sub + duc* (to conquer or control)

_____ **8.** *sub + port + ive* (giving help or strength)

_____ **9.** *in + duc* (to cause; to persuade)

_____ **10.** *trans + port + ion* (means of carrying goods or people from one place to another)

LESSON 21 continued

Spelling in Context

Write the word from the Word Bank that best fits in each sentence.

_____ **1.** Tai chi classes teach us to _____ ourselves with dignity.

_____ **2.** We learn to _____ our desire to rush.

_____ **3.** If we move too fast, we must _____ points from our total.

_____ **4.** Our instructor says that anxiety is _____.

_____ **5.** By focusing, we can _____ a state of calm.

Proofreading Practice

Read the paragraph. Find the five misspelled words and circle them. Then, on the numbered lines below, write the correct spelling for each circled word.

What kind of train carries a teacher instead of a conducor? Railroad cars provided education as well as transporrtation for Canadian children through the mid-twentieth century. Special cars became poartable classrooms, making annual visits to isolated areas. Suportive families shared food with the traveling teachers who lived onboard. Everyone worked to make the children's few weeks of school as produtive as possible.

1. _____   **3.** _____   **5.** _____

2. _____   **4.** _____

Spelling Application

Below are six more words that reflect the Key Concepts you have learned.

conducive   conduit   deduce   viaduct   portfolio   deportation

Do you speak Pig Latin? In this made-up "language," you take away the first letter of each word. You then add the letter to the extra syllable \ā\ at the end of the word. For example, Pig Latin becomes Ig-pay Atin-lay. "Translate" each Pig Latin word below. Write the English versions on the lines.

1. iaduct-vay   _____

2. educe-day   _____

3. onducive-cay   _____

4. ortfolio-pay   _____

5. onduit-cay   _____

6. eportation-day   _____

Spelling Power

Lesson 22: The Latin Word Roots *mort* and *vit/viv*

Word Bank

mortality	mortify	immortalize	vital	vitality
revive	survival	convivial	vivacious	vivacity

Key Concepts

1. The Latin word root *mort* means "death."
mortal: subject to death; earthly

2. The Latin word root *vit/viv* means "life."
vivid: bright; lively

Spelling Practice

Arrange the words from the Word Bank in alphabetical order. Write the words on the lines next to their meanings.

_____ **1.** sociable; the "life of the party"

_____ **2.** to give eternal life; to make famous

_____ **3.** death count; state of being subject to death

_____ **4.** to shame; to "embarrass to death"

_____ **5.** to return to life; to bring back to life

_____ **6.** remaining alive; outliving hardship or danger

_____ **7.** necessary to sustain life; of great importance

_____ **8.** energy; strength; health

_____ **9.** spirited; full of life

_____ **10.** liveliness; high spirits

Spelling in Context

Write the word from the Word Bank that best fits in each imaginary book title. Hint: Read the names of the authors carefully.

1. _____ *When Your Boat Sinks,* by Holger Breath

2. *How to* _____ *a Faded Romance,* by Hartz N. Flowerz

3. *How to* _____ *Your Neighbors,* by Hal O. Ween

4. _____ *Rates in this Century,* by Kick D. Buckett

5. *Recipes for* _____, by Lotta Veggies

LESSON 22 continued

Proofreading Practice

Read the paragraph. Find the five misspelled words and circle them. Then, on the numbered lines below, write the correct spelling for each circled word.

Mark Twain's novels immorrtalize his childhood home and companions. Tom Sawyer and Hannibal, Missouri, have become American icons. Adventure is vaital to Tom. His vyvacious ways frequently land him in trouble, and his wild escapades mourtify his aunt Polly. Tom's convevial nature leads him to include his friends in his adventures—and all readers imagine themselves to be Tom Sawyer's friends.

1. _____   4. _____

2. _____   5. _____

3. _____

Spelling Application

Listed below are five more words that reflect the Key Concepts you have learned. Use the words to fill in the crossword puzzle below.

mortally   mortician   conviviality   revitalize   vitamin

Across
4. If you have this trait, you love parties.
5. A person injured to this extent may die.

Down
1. Do this for a wilted plant, and it comes back to life.
2. This person prepares bodies for burial.
3. It's essential for health.

Spelling Power

Lesson 23: The Latin Word Roots *bene* and *mal*

Word Bank

maladjustment	malicious	malfunctioning	malady	malnourished
benefits	beneficial	benefactor	benevolent	benediction

Key Concepts

1. The Latin word root *bene* means "good" or "well."
   benign: harmless; kind

2. The Latin word root *mal/male* means "bad" or "badly."
   malice: spite; desire to do harm

Spelling Practice

Put the words from the Word Bank in alphabetical order. Hint: Their definitions are in order.

_____ **1.** a blessing

_____ **2.** a donor

_____ **3.** favorable; profitable

_____ **4.** advantages (n.); gives/receives advantages (v.)

_____ **5.** kind

_____ **6.** imbalance; faulty adjustment

_____ **7.** illness

_____ **8.** not functioning; functioning abnormally

_____ **9.** full of malice

_____ **10.** underfed; poorly nourished

Spelling in Context

Write the word that best completes each sentence.

_____ **1.** To fight the _____ known as muscular dystrophy, the Key Club held a jogathon.

_____ **2.** An anonymous _____ contributed $1,000.

_____ **3.** At the awards ceremony, the microphone began _____.

_____ **4.** A _____ of the lights left half the stage in shadow.

_____ **5.** Still the _____ nature of the cause kept everyone upbeat.

LESSON 23 continued

Proofreading Practice

Read the paragraph. Find the five misspelled words and circle them. Then, on the numbered lines below, write the correct spelling for each circled word.

The annual Feast of the Carrot benifits the town of Créances, France. This farming center is known for carrots that are so tasty and healthy that no one who eats them could possibly become mallnourished. Every August the members of the Brotherhood of Sand-grown Carrots parade through Créances in orange robes and green hats, celebrating the benificial qualities of their famous produce. No melicious mischief mars this unique country fair. A benadiction in the local church closes the festivities.

1. _____   4. _____

2. _____   5. _____

3. _____

Spelling Application

Listed below are six more words that reflect the Key Concepts you have learned. Write the word from the list that best answers each question.

beneficent   beneficiary   maleficent   malignant   malodorous   malpractice

_____ **1.** Which adjective could describe a person sprayed by a skunk?

_____ **2.** Of what would a health practitioner least want to be accused?

_____ **3.** Which noun refers to a person who benefits from another's insurance policy?

_____ **4.** Which adjective could describe a life-threatening tumor?

_____ **5.** Which adjective would be the greatest compliment to a public service worker?

_____ **6.** Which adjective would be the greatest insult to a public service worker?

Spelling Power

Lesson 24: Words Often Confused

Word Bank

alluding	ascent	eminent	epic	sight
eluding	assent	imminent	epoch	site

Key Concepts

There are many techniques that can help you to spell tricky word pairs. Two of these techniques are listed below:

1. Use memory aids.

stationery = paper

stationary = unable to move

2. Use your knowledge of roots and affixes.

immigrant = one who moves into a country (*in* + *migrant*)

emigrant = one who moves out of a country (*ex* + *migrant*)

Spelling Practice

Put the words from the Word Bank in alphabetical order. Hint: Their meanings and etymologies, or word origins, are already in correct order.

_____ **1.** making a sly or indirect reference (Latin *ad*, "toward" + *ludus*, "game")

_____ **2.** an upward motion (Latin *ad*, "toward" + *scandere*, "to climb")

_____ **3.** to agree (v.); agreement (n.) (Latin *ad*, "toward" + *sentire*, "to feel")

_____ **4.** escaping (Latin *e*, "out" + *ludus*, "game")

_____ **5.** outstanding (Latin *e*, "out" + *minere*, "to project")

_____ **6.** a long poem or tale (Greek *epikos*, "poem")

_____ **7.** an era of history (Greek *epokhe*, "pause")

_____ **8.** approaching; about to happen (Latin *in*, "inward" + *minere*, "to project")

_____ **9.** a view; (Old English *gesiht*, "vision")

_____ **10.** a place; a setting (Latin *situs*, "place")

LESSON 24 continued

Spelling in Context

Write the Word Bank word that best completes each sentence.

_____ **1.** Jamal reported on a(n) _____ poem from ancient Sumeria.

_____ **2.** The poem is set in the _____ when Ur was newly built.

_____ **3.** It tells of a hero's _____ into the mountains of the sun.

_____ **4.** He seeks the gods' _____ to restore his friend to life.

_____ **5.** The poem includes lines _____ to several Sumerian myths.

Proofreading Practice

Read the paragraph. Find the five misspelled or misused words and circle them. Then, on the numbered lines below, write the correct spelling for each circled word.

Where did Jamestown's colonists build their first fort? The exact sight was a mystery for centuries. Archaeologists searched, but success kept alluding them. In 1995, two emminent archaeologists dug on an island in Virginia's James River. Remains of rotting log walls told them that success was iminent. The site of skeletons and other remains from the 1607 settlement confirmed their find.

1. _____ **3.** _____ **5.** _____

2. _____ **4.** _____

Spelling Application

Listed below are eight more words that reflect the Key Concepts you have learned. Write the word from the list that best answers each riddle. Check a dictionary if you need help.

metal	mettle	chord	cord
descent	dissent	bazaar	bizarre

_____ **1.** I help you meet tough challenges. What am I?

_____ **2.** Girders and forks are made from me. What am I?

_____ **3.** You can buy various goods in me. What am I?

_____ **4.** Things like me are odd as can be. What am I?

_____ **5.** I may be a downward spiral. What am I?

_____ **6.** I say "NO"; I never agree. What am I?

_____ **7.** I'm one of the ties that bind. What am I?

_____ **8.** You hear me in melody and harmony. What am I?

Spelling Power

Unit 6: Review Lessons 21–24

allude	assent	benediction	benefactor	beneficial
comport	deducts	epic	epoch	imminent
induce	maladjustment	malicious	mortality	mortify
reduce	transportation	vitality	vivacious	vivacity

Write the words from the list above whose Latin word roots *bene* or *mal* have the meanings shown below.

well; good (*bene*)   bad; badly (*mal*)

1. _____   4. _____

2. _____   5. _____

3. _____

Write the words from the list above whose Latin word roots *mort* or *viv/vit* have the meanings shown below.

death (*mort*)   life (*viv/vit*)

6. _____   8. _____

7. _____   9. _____

10. _____

For each item, find the two words from the list above that best replace the words in parentheses. Write the words in the blanks that follow each sentence. Pay careful attention to words that are often confused.

11. Everyone felt sure the mayor's (agreement) was (upcoming).

_____ _____

12. Ada wrote her (long poem) about that (historical era).

_____ _____

13. If your dog wants to use public (ways of moving from place to place), the dog must know how to (behave) itself.

_____ _____

14. If John (removes) sweets from his diet, he will (become smaller) in size.

_____ _____

15. "Nothing you do can (cause) me to (refer to) my secret hideaway," proclaimed the captured pirate.

_____ _____

Spelling Power

Proofreading Application
Lessons 21–24

Read the Yellow Pages listings. Find the twenty misspelled words and circle them. Then, on the numbered lines below, write the correct spelling for each circled word.

Entertainment

Hot-Air Ballooning

Has excitement been alluding you lately? Come fly with us! Free trial assent every Monday morning! Rescue squad on sight. Friendly and suportive crew.
Phone 555-0703

Train Rides

Reviev memories of the old days with a ride on a real steam train. Enjoy the site of the puffing locomotive and see the caboose, where conducktor and crew could relax. Round-trip tour guided by imminent local historian.
Phone 555-4701

Services

Insurance

Worried about accidents, illness, or injuries due to mallfunctioning equipment? Don't neglect the vittal task of protecting yourself and your loved ones. Blue Nose insurance pays death benefits and covers medical costs in case of survivol. No maledy excluded from our Platinum Plan.
Phone 555-2813

Photography

Immortolize your family with professional photos by Blitz Brothers. With our "porttable studio," you can be photographed in the comfort of your home.
Phone 555-8030

Service Organizations

Want to do something prodoctive with your life? Aid the melnourished and suddue poverty—join the convilvial people in the Binevolent Society. Dinner meeting every Monday, 7:00 P.M., 479 Spring St. Bring a main dish and a $15.00 donation.
Phone 555-2773

1. _____
2. _____
3. _____
4. _____
5. _____
6. _____
7. _____
8. _____
9. _____
10. _____

11. _____
12. _____
13. _____
14. _____
15. _____
16. _____
17. _____
18. _____
19. _____
20. _____

Spelling Power

Lesson 25: Plurals of Nouns Ending in a Consonant + *o*

Word Bank

embargoes	mementos	virtuosos	commandos	placebos
dynamos	crescendos	ghettos	memos	fiascos

Key Concepts

1. Add *s* to form plurals of most nouns ending in a consonant + *o*.

   photos   logos

   pianos   tuxedos

2. Sometimes nouns ending in a consonant + *o* form their plurals by adding *es*.

   torpedoes   embargoes   heroes

   vetoes   echoes

   tomatoes   potatoes

Spelling Practice

Choose the word from the Word Bank that forms the plural of each noun listed below. Write your choices on the lines. Circle the word that ends in *es*.

_____ 1. embargo

_____ 2. dynamo

_____ 3. memento

_____ 4. crescendo

_____ 5. virtuoso

_____ 6. ghetto

_____ 7. commando

_____ 8. memo

_____ 9. placebo

_____ 10. fiasco

Spelling in Context

Write the plural noun that fits each definition and etymology (word origin).

_____ 1. inactive materials substituted for medicine (Latin *placebo,* "I will please")

_____ 2. severe trade restrictions (Spanish *embargo,* "I restrain")

_____ 3. increases in volume, building to a peak (Italian *crescendo,* "growing")

_____ 4. short notes used for business communications (Latin *memorandum,* "It is to be remembered")

_____ 5. electrical generators; high-energy people (Greek *dynamis,* "power")

Name _____ Date _____ Class _____

Proofreading Practice

Read the paragraph. Find the five misspelled nouns and circle them. Then, on the numbered lines below, write the correct spelling for each circled word.

   Mary McLeod Bethune was one of those remarkable people who might be called "classroom virtuosoes." She became a teacher because she wanted to free others from rural poverty and urban ghetto's. Her first attempts to found schools were almost fiascoes. She had no money and could build only in a city dump. She sent her students out like small commandose to scavenge for chairs. The charred sticks used as pencils might serve as mementoes of those years. Today her Bethune-Cookman College is a respected institution with a proud history.

1. _____ 3. _____ 5. _____

2. _____ 4. _____

Spelling Application

Below are six more nouns that reflect the Key Concepts you have learned. Use the wheel to decode the singular form of each noun. Write the singular and plural forms of each noun you have decoded.

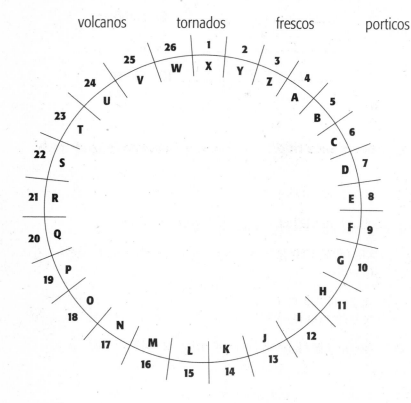

volcanos   tornados   frescos   porticos   staccatos   sopranos

1. 9-21-8-22-6-18
_____
_____

2. 22-23-4-6-6-4-23-18
_____
_____

3. 25-18-15-6-4-16-18
_____
_____

4. 23-18-21-17-4-7-18
_____
_____

5. 19-18-21-23-12-6-18
_____
_____

6. 22-18-19-21-4-17-18
_____
_____

Spelling Power

Lesson 26: Plurals of Nouns Ending in a Vowel + o

Word Bank

barrios	folios	pistachios	ratios	scenarios
cameos	duos	embryos	bamboos	tattoos

Key Concepts

Add s to form the plurals of words ending in a vowel + o.

trio + s = trios   taboo + s = taboos

Spelling Practice

For each term listed below, choose the word from the Word Bank that forms the plural. Write your choices on the lines.

_____ **1.** tattoo

_____ **2.** scenario

_____ **3.** embryo

_____ **4.** barrio

_____ **5.** duo

_____ **6.** ratio

_____ **7.** pistachio

_____ **8.** bamboo

_____ **9.** folio

_____ **10.** cameo

Spelling in Context

Write the word from the Word Bank that answers each riddle. Use the Key Concepts to spell each plural form correctly.

_____ **1.** We are neighborhoods rich in Hispanic culture. What are we?

_____ **2.** We express proportions in mathematical terms. What are we?

_____ **3.** We flavor ice cream. We're tasty green snacks, but sometimes we're dyed magenta. What are we?

_____ **4.** We may be brief appearances by actors, or we may be gems with raised carvings on contrasting backgrounds. What are we?

_____ **5.** We are sets of pages in a book or manuscript. What are we?

LESSON 26 continued

Proofreading Practice

Read the paragraph. Find the five misspelled words and circle them. Then, on the numbered lines below, write the correct spelling for each circled word.

   Furry black-and-white duoes clamber through the forests as raindrops mark their hides like tattoes. Here in China's Qin Ling mountains, giant pandas with cubs in tow graze among the bambooes. Few people witness scenarioes such as these, for only about a thousand giant pandas remain in the wild. Their birth rate has plunged, the embryoes apparently failing to implant after conception. Wildlife experts hope that newly expanded preserves will reverse the downward trend.

1. _____   3. _____   5. _____

2. _____   4. _____

Spelling Application

Below are five more words that reflect the Key Concepts you have learned. Read the definition of each word. Then list the words under the correct headings below. Hint: One of the words fits under two headings.

   adagios: slow sections of sonatas or concertos

   arpeggios: chords whose notes are played separately

   impresarios: those who sponsor and manage actors or musicians

   intaglios: engraved designs on paper, in stone, or on a jewel

   oratorios: musical dramas, usually based on religious texts and presented without costumes, scenery, or action

DRAMA	MUSIC	FINE ARTS

1. _____   3. _____   7. _____

2. _____   4. _____

                              5. _____

                              6. _____

Spelling Power

Lesson 27: Plurals of Nouns Ending in *s*, *ch*, *sh*, *x*, and *z*

Word Bank

witnesses	fortresses	wildernesses	backlashes	skirmishes
dispatches	monarchs	sphinxes	paradoxes	blitzes

Key Concepts

1. Add *es* to form plurals of most nouns ending in *s, x,* or *z*.

bypass + es = bypasses

fax + es = faxes

waltz + es = waltzes

2. Add *es* to form plurals of most nouns ending in *ch* or *sh*.

church + es = churches

marsh + es = marshes

3. Exceptions include any nouns whose final *ch* sounds like \k\:

stomach + s = stomachs

epoch + s = epochs

Spelling Practice

Choose the word from the Word Bank that forms the plural of each word below, and write your choice on the line. Then write the number of the Key Concept that applies to your choice.

Example: _epochs, 3_   epoch

_____ **1.** sphinx

_____ **2.** fortress

_____ **3.** paradox

_____ **4.** wilderness

_____ **5.** backlash

_____ **6.** dispatch

_____ **7.** witness

_____ **8.** blitz

_____ **9.** monarch

_____ **10.** skirmish

Spelling in Context

Write the word from the Word Bank closest in meaning to the nouns in each set. Write the plural form.

_____ **1.** messages, communications, bulletins

_____ **2.** strongholds, citadels, bastions

_____ **3.** reactions, repercussions, countermeasures

_____ **4.** clashes, scrimmages, scuffles

_____ **5.** bombardments, attacks, onslaughts

LESSON 27 continued

Proofreading Practice

Read the paragraph. Find the five misspelled words and circle them. Then, on the numbered lines below, write the correct spelling for each circled word.

A bright orange-and-black butterfly represents one of nature's paradoxs. How do monarchs, fragile as dry leaves, manage to migrate thousands of miles? Awed witnesss marvel each year as clouds of butterflies arrive at breeding grounds high in central Mexico's mountain wilderneses. How do these frail creatures find their way? Scientists are not sure. Mysterious as sphinxs, the butterflies keep their secrets.

1. _____   4. _____

2. _____   5. _____

3. _____

Spelling Application

Below are six more plural nouns that follow the patterns you have learned. Use the plural nouns to fill in the paragraph about Washington Irving's story "Rip Van Winkle."

abysses   blunderbusses   hoaxes   patriarchs   reproaches

In Irving's classic story, village (1) _____ gather at the local inn

to relax and talk. The action is set in the 1700s, when hunters still carry old-fashioned

(2) _____. Rip, a lazy and henpecked husband, literally heads for the

hills to escape the (3) _____ of his wife. He vanishes amid the mysterious

(4) _____ and peaks of the Catskill Mountains. Is Irving's tale of little men

of the mountains true, or is it one of his many (5) _____?

Spelling Power

Unit 7: Lesson 28: Plurals of Nouns Ending in *f* and *fe*

Word Bank

gulfs	shelves	beliefs	wolves	motifs
knives	takeoffs	proofs	scarves	sheaves

Key Concepts

1. Add *s* to form plurals of most nouns ending in *f*.

   cuff + s = cuffs   chief + s = chiefs

2. To form plurals of most nouns ending in *lf*, change *f* to *v* and add *es*.

   calf + es = calves   self + es = selves

3. To form plurals of some nouns ending in *rf*, either option is acceptable.

   dwarf + s = dwarfs *or* dwarf + es = dwarves

4. To form plurals of most nouns ending in *fe*, change *f* to *v* and add *s*.

   wife + s = wives

5. Exceptions to memorize:

   thief + es = thieves   leaf + es = leaves
   loaf + es = loaves   hoof + es = hooves
   sheaf + es = sheaves   gulf + s = gulfs

Spelling Practice

For each noun below, choose the word from the Word Bank that forms the plural. Write your choice on the line. Then write the number of the Key Concept that applies to your choice.

Example: wife   *wives, 4*

1. takeoff _____
2. belief _____
3. proof _____
4. motif _____
5. knife _____

6. wolf _____
7. shelf _____
8. scarf _____
9. gulf _____
10. sheaf _____

Spelling in Context

Form the plural of each word in parentheses. Use the Key Concepts to help you spell the words correctly.

1. Made out of wool, silk, cotton, or other material, (scarf) _____ wrap us up in all kinds of weather.

2. (Takeoff) _____ may be wild imitations, as well as the beginnings of vacations.

3. For photographers, (proof) _____ are work that is completed; for algebra buffs, they're ways to have fun.

LESSON 28 continued

4. (Motif) _____ are patterns found in parts of tales, songs, crafts, and other arts.

5. (Sheaf) _____ can be bundles of papers or grains.

Proofreading Practice

Read the paragraph. Find the five misspelled words and circle them. Then, on the numbered lines below, write the correct spelling for each circled word.

On April 1, 1999, Canada created its newest territory, Nunavut. There, north of the Arctic Circle, more than twenty thousand Inuit bridge the many gulves between ancient beliefes and modern ways of life. Inuit hunters may use snowmobiles instead of dogsleds, but they still follow tradition to maintain the natural balance between wolfs and caribou. Their hunting camps may feature tents and sleeping bags instead of igloos with sleeping shelffs, but they still use traditional curved knifes to prepare their catch.

1. _____ **3.** _____ **5.** _____

2. _____ **4.** _____

Spelling Application

Below are ten nouns whose plurals are found using the Key Concepts you have learned. Fill in the blank spaces in the puzzle. The circled letters will show the answer to this riddle:

Why do surgeons make good comedians?

Because they leave you __ __ __ __ __ __ __ __ __ . __ __ __.

cliffs	lift-offs	tariffs	reliefs	lives
skiffs	spin-offs	reefs	spoofs	halves

1. __ k ◯ __ __ __   **6.** ◯ __ __ i __ __ __

2. __ p __ ◯ - __ __ __ __   **7.** ◯ __ i __ __ __

3. __ __ __ o __ ◯   **8.** ◯ a __ __ __ __

4. __ __ __ ◯ - o __ __ __   **9.** r __ ◯ __ __

5. __ __ l ◯ __ __ __   **10.** __ i __ __ ◯

Name _____ Date _____ Class _____

Spelling Power

Unit 7: Review Lessons 25–28

backlashes	barrios	beliefs	blitzes	commandos
dispatches	embargoes	embryos	folios	ghettos
knives	mementos	motifs	pistachios	placebos
proofs	sheaves	sphinxes	tattoos	witnesses

From the word list above, select the word that best completes each sentence. Write the word in the blank.

1. My favorite nuts are not almonds, but _____.

2. Molly has very strong _____ about the importance of hard work.

3. How many _____ do we need to cut these apples?

4. Tim wanted to remember his visit to France, so he kept many _____ from his trip.

5. "I said blintzes, not _____," the customer told the waiter.

6. In Spanish-speaking countries, neighborhoods are called _____.

7. In order to catch the thief, police had to interview many _____.

8. After the harvest, wheat is gathered and bundled into _____.

9. It takes nine months for human _____ to develop.

10. Some dogs now have their skin marked with identification _____ so that they can be returned to their owners if lost.

Use the remaining words from the word list to write ten sentences of your own.

11. _____
12. _____
13. _____
14. _____
15. _____
16. _____
17. _____
18. _____
19. _____
20. _____

Proofreading Application

Lessons 25–28
Read the following brochure. Find the twenty misspelled words and circle them. Then, on the numbered lines below, write the correct spelling for each circled word.

Visit Plenty-O-Playlands Park!

Land-O-Adventures
Explore fortresss in vast wildernesss. Witness skirmishs between powerful monarches and armored knights. Sail across stormy gulves to wild islands—but beware of wolfes and other wild creatures! You might even glimpse tigers slipping between the tall bambooes.

Land-O-Performers
Work with real comedians, doing takeoves and slapstick scenarioes. Be on the lookout for famous stars stopping in for cameoes with you! Learn "Transforming Scarfes" and other tricks from professional magicians. Sing or play music with virtuosoes; let your performances build to crescendoes. Don't worry about stage fright; there are never any fiascoes at Plenty-O-Playlands!

Land-O-Discoveries
Build electrical dynamoes. Puzzle over the paradoxs of physics. Explore the ratioes and progressions of natural processes. As partners in discovery duoes, you'll have access to limitless shelfes of science equipment and supplies, in addition to careful guidance from working scientists. Take home a record of your discoveries—photos and memoes signed by our staff of professionals.

1. _____
2. _____
3. _____
4. _____
5. _____
6. _____
7. _____
8. _____
9. _____
10. _____

11. _____
12. _____
13. _____
14. _____
15. _____
16. _____
17. _____
18. _____
19. _____
20. _____

Name _____ Date_____ Class _____

Spelling Power

Lesson 29: Unusual Plurals

Word Bank

stimulus	antenna	memorandum	phenomenon	hypothesis
stimuli	antennae	memoranda	phenomena	hypotheses

Key Concepts

Nouns from Greek or Latin may have unusual singular and plural forms.

1. Use the following pattern for nouns ending in *is* and for some nouns ending in *x*.

   crisis ⇒ crises

   index ⇒ indices

2. Use the following patterns for many nouns ending in *us*, *a*, *um*, or *on*.

   fungus ⇒ fungi

   larva ⇒ larvae

   datum ⇒ data

   criterion ⇒ criteria

Spelling Practice

Write the words from the Word Bank in alphabetical order. After each word, write *S* for singular or *P* for plural. Then write the number of the Key Concept that applies to that word.

Example: datum   data, P, 2

1. _____   6. _____
2. _____   7. _____
3. _____   8. _____
4. _____   9. _____
5. _____   10. _____

Spelling in Context

Write the word that fits in each sentence. Be sure to use the correct singular or plural ending.

_____ 1. A _____ alerted staff to the problem at the broadcasting studio.

_____ 2. The main _____ was not functioning correctly.

_____ 3. The maintenance crew had several _____ about the cause of the problem.

_____ 4. They put up two temporary _____ to keep the station on the air.

_____ 5. During the week, a series of _____ reported on the progress of the repair effort.

LESSON 29 continued

Proofreading Practice

Read the paragraph. Find the five misspelled nouns and circle them. Then, on the numbered lines below, write the correct spelling for each circled word.

Did you know that some animals have built-in magnets? Scientists studying the phenomenen of animal migration have recently proven that hypothesus. Migrating animals seem to be guided by many stimuluses, including the position of the sun and the patterns of the stars. The single most important stimulis, however, comes from within: magnetic sensors in these animals' brains work like compass needles. Phenomenae such as these make the life sciences fascinating.

1. _____   4. _____

2. _____   5. _____

3. _____

Spelling Application

Listed below are five more singular nouns. Write these nouns in the first column. Then write the plural form of each word in the second column. Use a dictionary if necessary.

analysis   curriculum   diagnosis   medium   vortex

Singular   **Plural**

1. _____   _____

2. _____   _____

3. _____   _____

4. _____   _____

5. _____   _____

Spelling Power

Lesson 30: Spelling Possessive Forms

Word Bank

discovery's	helix's	radius's	alumna's	yours
discoveries'	helices'	radii's	alumnae's	theirs

Key Concepts

1. Add apostrophe + *s* to form the possessive of most singular nouns.

boy ⟹ boy's

cactus ⟹ cactus's

2. Add only an apostrophe to form the possessive of plural nouns ending in *s.*

boys ⟹ boys'

recipes ⟹ recipes'

3. Add apostrophe + *s* to form the possessive of plural nouns that do not end in *s.*

children ⟹ children's

cacti ⟹ cacti's

4. Never add apostrophes to possessive forms of personal pronouns.

you ⟹ yours   our ⟹ ours

they ⟹ theirs   it ⟹ its

Spelling Practice

For each noun below, choose the word from the Word Bank that forms the possessive. Write your choices on the lines.

_____ **1.** radius

_____ **2.** helix

_____ **3.** alumnae

_____ **4.** discoveries

_____ **5.** radii

_____ **6.** discovery

_____ **7.** alumna

_____ **8.** helices

Choose the words that form the possessives of the pronouns.

_____ **9.** you

_____ **10.** they

Spelling in Context

Write the possessive form that best fits in each sentence.

_____ **1.** To find the area of a circle, you need to know the _____ length.

_____ **2.** The areas of two circles are equal if their _____ lengths are equal.

_____ **3.** One Harvard _____ major was physics.

_____ **4.** Several other _____ majors were mathematics.

_____ **5.** The scientific world exclaimed the _____ uniqueness.

LESSON 30 continued

Proofreading Practice

Read the paragraph. Find the five misspelled possessive nouns and pronouns and circle them. Then, on the numbered lines below, write the correct spelling for each circled word.

> Sunflowers, pine cones, and your DNA—what do they have in common? Their design follows a helixs pattern, a spiral coil. The helice's shapes may vary—one flat, one a cone, one a cylinder—but the basic spiral remains. The structure that is their's is also your's. Fibonacci of Pisa, a thirteenth-century mathematician, found a number sequence that underlies these helices. His discoverys significance is vast. Fibonacci's sequence recurs in sciences ranging from genetics to quantum physics—sciences not even known in his lifetime.

1. _____   4. _____

2. _____   5. _____

3. _____

Spelling Application

Listed below are five more possessive nouns and pronouns that reflect the Key Concepts you have learned. Use the possessives to complete the imaginary business addresses below. Hint: Read the entire address carefully, including the state abbreviation.

ours   its   women's   showoff's   comedians'

Exercise and _____ Benefits
Sports Equipment Store
123 Runnina Circle
Friss, KY

The Stars Are _____
Model Rocketry Supplies
6543 Two Run
Zeer, OH

Monkey Business
_____ Supplies
222 Zaney Way
Maney, AK

A _____ Delight
Theater Props and Costumes
2 Broad Way
Lookit, ME

Elegant _____ Clothing
4 Saxfifth Avenue
Supeery, OR

Spelling Power

Lesson 31: Compounds

Word Bank

halfhearted	peacekeeping	full-blown	all-terrain	self-confidence
ex-president	matter-of-fact	secretary-general	best-seller	all right

Key Concepts

1. Compounds can be closed, hyphenated, or open.

back + board = backboard

time + out = time-out

free + throw = free throw

Note: Add hyphens to open compounds used as adjectives.

Take a free throw.

Stand at the free-throw line.

2. Keep all the letters in both words when forming closed compounds—even if the results look odd.

high + light = highlight

busy + body = busybody

book + bag = bookbag

3. Hyphenate most compounds with *self-, ex-, full-, part-,* and *great-.*

self + reliant = self-reliant

Spelling Practice

Put the words from the Word Bank in alphabetical order. Write the words on the lines below.

1. _____

2. _____

3. _____

4. _____

5. _____

6. _____

7. _____

8. _____

9. _____

10. _____

Spelling in Context

Write the compound that fits in each sentence.

1. Have you read *Markings*, by Dag Hammarskjold, former _____ of the United Nations?

2. Hammerskjold's approach to his difficult job was anything but _____.

3. After his death, the book—which had been taken from his journals—became a _____.

4. It expresses his deep doubts as well as his _____.

5. He maintained hope that even the world's toughest problems could come out _____.

LESSON 31 continued

Proofreading Practice

Read the paragraph. Find the five misspelled compounds and circle them. Then, on the numbered lines below, write the correct spelling for each circled compound.

Between 1950 and 1953, American soldiers made up the bulk of U.N. troops in troubled South Korea. What had begun as a peace keeping mission soon erupted into full blown war. Using tanks and other allterrain vehicles, American troops fought bravely to aid South Koreans. Years later, exPresident Harry Truman stated in his matter of fact way that sending American troops to Korea had been the toughest decision of his career.

1. _____   **4.** _____

2. _____   **5.** _____

3 _____

Spelling Application

Listed below are five more compounds that reflect the Key Concepts you have learned. Write the best compound to complete each analogy.

foolhardy   full-time   outer space   well-being   well-to-do

1. poor : _____ :: sweet : sour

2. whirlpool : ocean :: black hole : _____

3. _____ : reckless :: prudent : careful

4. part-time : _____ :: fraction : whole

5. satisfaction : discontentment :: _____ : misery

Spelling Power

Lesson 32: Easily Misspelled Words

Word Bank

persistent	braggart	negligent	mystical	artisan
recuperate	detached	articulate	myriad	imperative

Key Concepts

To learn to spell a tricky word, use four steps:

1. Pronounce the word aloud. Notice how its letters relate to its sounds.
2. Close your eyes and picture the word.
3. Copy the word twice.
4. Write the word once without looking at the list. Check your spelling. If you find errors, repeat Steps 1–3.

Spelling Practice

Choose the Word Bank word that fits each pronunciation. Write your choices on the lines.

_____ 1. \ri kōō′ pə rāt\

_____ 2. \di tacht′\

_____ 3. \im per′ ə tiv\

_____ 4. \är′ tə zən\

_____ 5. \brag′ ərt\

_____ 6. \är tik′ yə lit\

_____ 7. \pər sis′ tənt\

_____ 8. \mis′ ti kəl\

_____ 9. \neg′ li jənt\

_____ 10. \mir′ ē əd\

Spelling in Context

Write the word from the Word Bank that fits in each sentence.

_____ 1. Successful debaters must be _____ and well-prepared.

_____ 2. Was Lisa being a _____ when she said our team was sure to win?

_____ 3. A _____ observer might have thought so.

_____ 4. We were never _____ in our preparation or practice.

_____ 5. After winning the trophy, we took a day off to _____.

LESSON 32 continued

Proofreading Practice

Read the paragraph. Find the five misspelled words and circle them. Then, on the numbered lines below, write the correct spelling for each circled word.

A century ago, Antonio Gaudí created what may be the world's most beautiful playground. More than an artisin, this architect and artist built his Parc Güell in the hills of Barcelona, Spain. The park includes miriad sculptures and mystycal spaces to explore. For Gaudí, achieving a blend of imagination and practicality was imperitive. His persistant efforts resulted in a public garden that is also a spectacular work of art.

1. _____   4. _____

2. _____   5. _____

3 _____

Spelling Application

Listed below are six more words that are easily misspelled. Follow the four steps listed in the Key Concepts to learn to spell each word. Then write the word that fits in each tongue twister.

familiar   minuscule   obnoxious   optimism   sarcasm   sherbet

1. Sherm's _____ sure seems sugary.

2. The apt _____ missed Oliver Olsen.

3. Four _____ fiddlers flew in five fiddles from Florida.

4. Meet Mild Milly, the _____ milliner.

5. Samson's _____ has Sad Sam sick!

6. _____ oxen auction socks.

Spelling Power

Unit 8: Review Lessons 29–32

all right	alumna's	antenna	antennae	articulate
detached	ex-president	full-blown	helices'	helix's
imperative	memorandum	myriad	peacekeeping	radii's
radius's	recuperate	secretary-general	stimuli	stimulus

From the word list above, select the words that best complete each sentence. Write the words in the blanks.

1. This insect is missing an _____. All of the other insects have two

   _____.

2. Begin the experiment by applying one _____, such as light. Over time you may test

   the effects of other _____, such as sound and heat.

3. By measuring one _____ length in a circle, you can learn all

   _____ lengths for that same circle.

4. The _____, who acts as a chief administrative officer, may be involved in a

   _____ mission to encourage peace in other countries.

5. Looking at the pictures in the science textbook, Suzy examined the _____ spiral form.

   She then became interested in the many other_____ forms pictured in the book.

For each phrase below, write the word from the list above that best fits the phrase.

6. "memo" is the abbreviated form   _____

7. everything correct   _____

8. former company leader   _____

9. completely developed   _____

10. belonging to a female graduate   _____

11. "You must!"   _____

12. speak well, or explain   _____

13. many   _____

14. get well   _____

15. not attached   _____

Spelling Power

Proofreading Practice

Read the following yearbook autographs. Find the twenty misspelled words and circle them. Then, on the numbered lines below, write the correct spelling for each circled word.

- To the lab partner who helped me observe every phenomena, test every hypothosis, and analyze every discoverys' meaning . . . how did we survive?

- Hold on to that selfconfidence—you're bound to write a best seller one of these days!

- Remember the mystocal moebius strips in math class? Why didn't ours turn out like their's?

- I vote you most likely to end up driving an all terrain vehicle!

- To the master of matter of fact statements, from the wizard of wild memorandae.

- According to all my hypotheses', your many discoverys' fame will last a thousand years!

- You were never a braggert; you were never neglagent; you were never half-hearted; you were always persistant—and you finally graduated, you lucky dog!

- Those jump shots of your's are major phenomenas—way to go!

- To the artisen who made the centerpieces for the alumnas's tea, from the cook who made the cookies.

1. _____
2. _____
3. _____
4. _____
5. _____
6. _____
7. _____
8. _____
9. _____
10. _____

11. _____
12. _____
13. _____
14. _____
15. _____
16. _____
17. _____
18. _____
19. _____
20. _____